MONADNOCK SUMMER

W ILLIAM M ORGAN

MONADNOCK SUMMER

The Architectural Legacy of Dublin, New Hampshire

D AVID R. G ODINE

Publisher · Boston

First published in 2011 by
David R. Godine, Publisher
Post Office Box 450
Jaffrey, New Hampshire 03452
www.godine.com

LIBRARY OF CONGRESS
CATALOGING-IN-PUBLICATION DATA

Morgan, William, 1944–
Monadnock summer : the architectural legacy of Dublin, New Hampshire /
by William Morgan.
   p.   cm.
Includes bibliographical references.
ISBN-13: 978-1-56792-422-0
ISBN-10: 1-56792-422-0
1. Architecture—New Hampshire—Dublin. 2. Historic buildings—
New Hampshire—Dublin. 3. Dublin (N.H.)—Buildings, structures, etc.
I. Title. II. Title: Architectural legacy of Dublin, New Hampshire.
NA735.D79M67 2011
720.9742'9—dc22
2010046277

FIRST EDITION
Printed in China

PAGE 1: *Scully garage*
FRONTISPIECE: *View of Dublin, c.1895*

CONTENTS

The Publisher would like to thank
the Dublin Historical Society for
the generous support it has provided
for the production and printing
of MONADNOCK SUMMER.

Dublin is the one place I have always longed for,
but never knew it existed in fact until now.

MARK TWAIN

Dedication

to WILLIAM L. BAUHAN

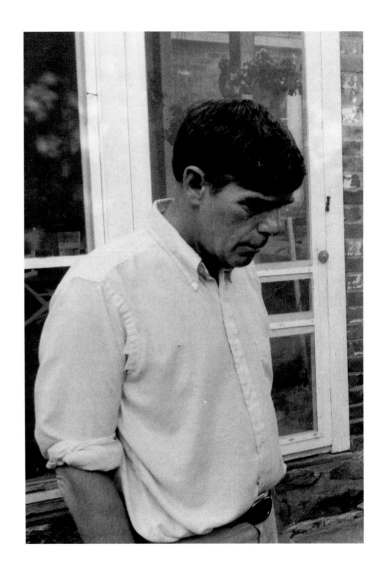

WILLIAM L. BAUHAN'S unequalled knowledge of Dublin history and his love of the town permeate this book.

Bill Bauhan was instrumental in the revival of the Dublin Historical Society in 1986 and served as president for its fledgling year. But this book has its origins in Bill's larger role as chronicler of Dublin's architecture. Ten years earlier, he initiated a survey of the town's buildings. This took the form of a questionnaire to homeowners, asking about the date of their houses, previous owners, and any special design or historical features. Many of the blanks were filled in by Bauhan himself, the authority of first and last resort for anyone trying to learn anything about a Dublin dwelling or family.

The buildings survey became the basis of a sprawling nomination to the National Register of Historic Places. Under Bauhan's leadership, an astonishing 156 individual buildings and two historic districts were accepted by the Department of Interior in 1983. When Dublin was threatened by a Route 101 bypass, one New Hampshire transportation official remarked that Dublin was perhaps the most thoroughly researched town in the state. Whether being on the National Register could have forestalled an asphalt-clad invader, as some anti-highway advocates hoped, the comprehensive nomination certainly highlighted the fact that Dublin's architecture was of national significance.

As the sage of Dublin, Bill Bauhan is so identified with its history that it is easy to forget that he was not a native, and that his journey to his spiritual home passed through many intriguing places.

William Lathrop Bauhan was born in Princeton, New Jersey, in 1929, where his father was a successful architect working primarily in the Colonial Revival style. Rolf W. Bauhan was among the first graduates of the architecture program at Princeton, and following service in World War I, was part of the team that rebuilt Soissons Cathedral in France. Bill's mother, Libbett, was the daughter of William Lathrop, an American Impressionist considered the founder of the artists' colony in New Hope, Pennsylvania. His parents moved from Princeton to an eighteenth-century Bucks County stone farmhouse outside New Hope where Bill attended the Solebury School, which was founded by his uncle, Julian Lathrop. Rolf Bauhan converted the buildings on another old farm to academic use.

Bill discovered the Monadnock region as a teenager, when he was invited to Newt and Janet Tolman's in Nelson. A painter, Janet was also from Bucks County, Pennsylvania. Like his father, Bill attended Princeton, where he majored in history and wrote his thesis on early town planning in Keene. The area lured him back after service in the army (he learned Russian and was stationed along the Czech border near the medieval city of Fulda) and study at St. Catherine's College, Oxford. In England he met and married Elizabeth Forbes, who had been born on a tea plantation in India.

Bill purchased a small publishing company, and he and Liz moved to New Hampshire – first to Jaffrey, then to Dublin (to a windswept mountainside house they dubbed Wuthering

Heights), and on to Noone House in Peterborough, where their children Patrick and Sarah were born. The Bauhans were involved in the life of "Our Town," and Bill was instrumental in pioneering preservation efforts there, implementing Peterborough's first architectural survey, a task that he would repeat a few years later in neighboring Dublin.

The family and business moved to the Alexander James house in Dublin's Lower Village in 1972, and in some ways it seemed that Bill had always been there. At both Noone House in Peterborough and at Home James in Dublin, Liz and Bill Bauhan ran what might be called a salon. The tone was set by a comfortable house, filled with paintings by one of America's outstanding landscape painters, mountains of books, a sophisticated garden, and a menagerie of cats and dogs, most of them rescued. The Bauhan home was a hospice that would have made St. Francis proud.

The whole ambience was tremendously appealing, exciting even, like visiting Emerson in nineteenth-century Concord or hanging out at Shakespeare & Company in Paris in the 1920s. You never knew who might end up sharing a meal with you: a poet, a writer, a preservationist, a bagpiper, a relative from Colorado, a classmate from Turkey – any and all were welcome, particularly if they partook of the life of the academy, the studio, or the spirit. Time spent at the Bauhans was better than any classroom – and a lot more fun. It almost always meant an impromptu exploratory trip – to the top of Newt Tolman's mountain in Nelson, to an orchestra concert or a contra dance in a nearby meetinghouse, and

certainly to scope out an historic house where some bygone literary light had once summered.

Bill's kitchen table was the special command center from which emanated this intellectual electricity. There, with a view of the garden, amid teetering stacks of newspapers, cookbooks, and biographies of English monarchs, Bill mobilized the forces of civilization. If there was anyone who exemplified the phrase "think globally, act locally," it was Bill Bauhan. His mind embraced the world, but his field of action lay at the foot of Mount Monadnock.

Bill had a corporate office in the barn where he published books and, the hope was, he would earn the wherewithal to support the important business of his life, which was friendship, family, and not least of all Dublin. The publishing business was remarkably successful in the ultimate meaning of the craft. Beginning with very limited resources and wanting to do only a certain kind of book, Bill made it work: he was editor, designer, warehouse manager, and publicity department. A one-man publishing outfit doesn't make any economic sense – unless you want total control of the product. Bauhan did not ever produce an unattractive book. Year after year, Bill increased our knowledge of New England history, revived worthy artists' reputations, and gave us decent poetry – all while unswervingly adhering to an old fashioned standard of quality. This was no mean achievement.

Like Bill, I too, grew up in Princeton and New Hope and our families were intertwined over several generations. But I really became part of the Bauhan coterie following a visit to Noone House while on a college tour in 1961. From then on, until Bill's death forty-five years later, I came to Peterborough and then to Dublin as often as I could. Such visits would often include learning about Raphael Pumpelly or the British summer embassy on Snow Hill, tales of who was related to whom, and the obligatory drive through the Latin Quarter.

The first event I ever attended in Dublin was a cocktail party at the Stone House in about 1963. The doyenne of the summer colony, and a living link to its golden age, Mrs. Joseph Lindon Smith – Aunt Corinna – was holding court. Thomas Handasyd Cabot, the son-in-law of the painter George de Forest Brush and the architect of the house was there also. It was a perfect autumn day. It was easy for an impressionable college student to be bowled over by Dublin's heady, even exotic, cultural scene.

As the architectural historian Bill knew best (and one he might like to have hanging around the kitchen), I was hired to prepare Peterborough's architectural survey in the early 1970s. The Peterborough survey was done while I was teaching at Princeton – a five-hour drive away. When it came time to work on the Dublin National Register project, I was living in Louisville, Kentucky – a much longer trek. Even so, there was never any question of not helping Bill document his beloved Dublin. I came when I could, and dragged my family to Dublin for several summers.

It was when we were renting what had been George Grey Barnard's daughter's studio on Learned Road that Bill and I first discussed the idea of a book about Dublin's architectural legacy. The architectural quality of the houses we were considering, as well as the depth of their historical associations, all shouted that here was a story that needed telling.

The art of architecture is often exciting, but books about it rarely are. So Bill imagined a book that would include the people and events that took place within those houses – a social and cultural history. Since this was Bill's bailiwick, he began to flesh out my rather spare skeleton into a whole body of knowledge about Dublin. We got more than halfway. Then life intervened. I wrote other books, and he published other titles. Subsequently, a new town history, as well as one on the Dublin Lake Club, appeared. Liz died in 1990, and then Bill followed her in 2006.

So *Monandock Summer* is not Bill's social history. Rather, it is an overview of Dublin's architectural legacy. But I am standing on William L. Bauhan's shoulders – this could not have been written without relying on his work. His National Register entries, the unpublished bits of the dreamed-of book, and the memories of decades of conversations about Dublin are all interwoven here. Let this volume be another chapter of Bill Bauhan's legacy to the place he so cherished.

Introduction

THE SETTING

Dublin's destiny has been determined by one dominant geographic feature: Mount Monadnock. That freestanding peak, along with the lake at its northern base, remains the most abiding image of Dublin. The mountain defined its growth and shaped its identity. The Native Americans venerated the mountain, while it inspired more artists and writers than any other peak in New England. The town's setting may appear idyllic, but the land was inhospitable, and Dublin was long isolated from the rest of the world.

Dublin was granted as "Monadnock No. 3" in 1749, the same year that the Boston publication "Summary Historical and Political of the First Planting of the British Settlements in No. America" carried the earliest printed mention of Mount Monadnock. Various eighteenth-century trails connected Portsmouth and Boston with Vermont and Fort Ticonderoga, but roads through Dublin came much later.

New Hampshire's Masonian Proprietors – Portsmouth land speculators – made the initial Dublin grants to individual landowners. The town (which included the southern half of what is now Harrisville) was divided into two hundred lots of roughly a hundred acres each, none of which was settled by the original grantees, whose interest was purely speculative. The largest landowner was Dr. Matthew Thornton (later a signer of the Declaration of Independence), but his brother Col. William Thornton was the first settler in 1752. Fear of Indian attacks made his stay in Dublin short.

Dublin was officially chartered in 1771, although groups of English settlers from Massachusetts and some Scotch-Irish from eastern New Hampshire arrived here about 1760. One of these, Henry Strongman, was likely born in Dublin, Ireland, and thus allegedly named the town in honor of his birthplace. On the eve of the American Revolution the town had a sawmill, a gristmill, a rude meetinghouse and a minister, as well as a population of 305. Following independence, some veterans purchased land in Dublin, but this was an unpromising, back-of-beyond agricultural town.

The story of Dublin's architecture thus begins simultaneously with the founding of the new republic.

Chapter One

EARLY ARCHITECTURE

HENRY DAVID THOREAU, while on a walking trip to Mount Monadnock in 1852, stopped at a house situated on the east flank of the mountain. The simple frame cottage where Thoreau tarried for a drink of cider was then only about thirty years old. The owner who chatted with the author and naturalist that September afternoon was the second generation of his family to live there. Joseph Eveleth's father, Joab, had built the house on land given to him by his brother-in-law at the time of his marriage into the locally prominent Gowing family.

It is unlikely that the Transcendentalist philosopher took much notice of the story-and-a-half center chimney house with its narrow clapboards and asymmetrical fenestration, nor gave any thought to a similar farmhouse down the road. Had he asked, he would have learned that the Samuel Snow farm was three decades older than the Eveleths.[1] Thoreau would have been more taken with the sweeping view eastward from Monadnock to the Peterborough Hills, although he might have shown polite interest in the fact that Abbott Bowman Burpee, a successful farmer known for his apples, eggs, celery, and of course cider, had just bought the Snow property.

For the inveterate traveler and journal maker, two examples of New England's vernacular house type would have been no more exciting than gazing upon a suburban ranch house of our time. Yet these two houses are surviving and well-preserved examples of what was the most common domestic dwelling of Dublin's early years. The very first set-tlers sheltered themselves from the elements in caves dug into hillsides or in primitive tents or log cabins. But none of these habitations remains, whereas cottages of the post-Revolutionary period are well represented.

ABOVE: *Eveleth/Thoreau Cottage*
OPPOSITE: *Mount Monadnock and the Snow Cottage*

These first permanent dwellings are often called Cape Cod cottages. That ubiquitous New England building type remained popular in Dublin for almost a century. Their chief characteristics are the two-room plan, central chimney, single-story configuration (with half or attic story above),

steep roofs, narrow windows, and frame construction.[2] Successive owners have altered almost all of these early cottages, but the plain one built by Revolutionary War veteran Solomon Piper in 1794 for his wife Susanna and their ten children at the lower end of Valley Road is as an example of this early type.

Although sources of Dublin's early houses may be discerned in distant echoes of the unpretentious, late-Medieval cottages of rural England, their simple forms were based more on practical considerations than on the remembrance of the homes the settlers' parents and grandparents left behind in the British Isles. Henry Strongman's house of around 1770 is also a Cape.

Despite the continued popularity of the cottage form, more formal and classically inspired houses were built in Dublin almost from the beginning. The town's population had tripled to 901 by the time of the nation's first census in 1790. These dwellings reflect the town's growth, as well as a certain post-Revolutionary War stability under the Federalists. As a hinterland, Dublin was stylistically far behind the coastal regions of New England, and few of these structures are comparable to the Renaissance-inspired Georgian. Yet, even in their crude regional fashion, Dublin's larger houses express the aesthetic aspirations of a frontier village that was slowly emerging from a hardscrabble subsistence.

The evolution from settlers concerned only with shelter to a class of housewrights is embodied by the Greenwood family, a local dynasty of carpenters and masons, one of

ABOVE: *Franklin Bond House*
RIGHT: *Abijah Richardson House*
OPPOSITE: *Snow Farm*

William and Joshua Greenwood House

whom, Moses, built the Town Pound in 1790, a thirty-foot-square, six-foot-high stone pen for stray animals that still stands. William Greenwood, an original immigrant from Sherborn, Massachusetts, was in the midst of building his substantial residence in 1782 when he was killed during the raising of his neighbor Benjamin Learned's barn. His son Joshua, also a carpenter (and known as "Wooden Josh" to differentiate him from his blacksmith cousin "Iron Josh"), completed the house. The result epitomizes the rectangular New England house with a central door.

Framed with oak trees felled on the property, it is a 42-by-32-foot structure with a massive chimney and symmetrical fenestration. Its sole adornment is a Federal-style doorway with an elliptical fan, added about 1837 by Rufus Piper, Joshua Greenwood's grandson and the fourth generation of carpenter builders.

The Isaac Appleton house, built on the Hancock Road about 1785 by a veteran of the Revolution and town moderator, is similar to the nearly square central-chimney houses erected in Dublin at this time, except that its detailing and symmetry exhibit a vague recollection of the sophisticated seacoast Georgian. Here a subtle proportional relationship is achieved by the fenestration: the second story windows are not only smaller than those on the first floor, but have 12-over-8 sashes instead of the 12-over-12 below. The chief glory of the house is the central doorway, which is flanked by Tuscan pilasters supporting a full entablature and a triangular pediment.

Another landmark of the period is the Old Tavern House, or Chamberlain's Tavern, a structure that served as the village's social and commercial hub from its construction in 1797 until its transformation into a private residence in 1835. Dublin's oldest hotel was also its first post office, as well as the home of the region's earliest gathering of Masons, the Altemont Lodge. The publican was Cyrus Chamberlain, who also served as postmaster, town clerk, and librarian of the Dublin Social Library.[3]

When the old tavern was moved in 1852 to make way for the construction of the third meetinghouse, its central chimney was removed, the 12-over-12 sashes were replaced with 6-over-6, and a Greek revival doorway was added. Yet the house retains its exquisite proportions, demonstrating the pervading balance and symmetry of the Georgian period. The low, hipped roof shows the transition to the Federal style, but the giant corner pilasters are hallmarks of the mid-eighteenth century in New England.

The increasing sophistication found in Dublin's generally plain eighteenth-century architectural legacy reveals a certain yeoman prosperity. The modest wealth of the post-Revolutionary period is illustrated in certain refinements that can be seen as local variants of the Federal style. An American reflection of English neoclassicism, Federal – or late Georgian – is often regarded as a high-water mark of New England design.[4]

With the early years of the nineteenth century came lower pitched roofs, increasingly refined proportional rela-

Isaac Appleton House

tionships, and Roman details revived by the Brothers Adam in Britain – albeit later and more conservatively in Dublin than elsewhere in New England. Despite President Jefferson's economically damaging trade embargo against Britain in 1806 and the agriculturally disastrous snow-filled summer of 1816, Dublin achieved a population of 1260 by 1820,

TOP: *Chamberlain's Tavern*
ABOVE: *Eli Morse House*
OPPOSITE: *Rufus Piper House*

a figure that would not be surpassed for a century and a half. That constancy is apparent in the town's few examples of the Federal style.

Federal builders were seemingly more interested in pleasing the eye than in holding the rigorous climate at bay. One feature of this trend towards elegance was the employment of an elliptical fan or fanlight above the entrance. Fanlights and other Adamesque details were made both popular and accessible by the hugely successful pattern books of Boston architect Asher Benjamin; these were written for untrained carpenter-builders and effectively disseminated the Boston high style into the hinterlands of northern New England.

Much of the Federal style in Dublin is attributed to Rufus Piper, the carpenter (and undertaker) who served the village as town moderator, justice of the peace, and Commander of the Dublin Grenadiers. Piper added a number of fans to various houses in town, including his own home on Pierce Road and his grandfather's on Main Street.

Joseph Hayward's 1794 house was built of brick, and the increasing use of masonry during this period is another indicator of Dublin's relative prosperity. A number of brick houses were built between 1820 and 1836, five of which survive. The substantial house that Thaddeus Morse added to his father Eli's cottage at the end of the lake in 1822 is a classic example of the regional Federal style.[5]

The original section of the Morse house, built c. 1760, was the site of the first sermon preached in Dublin in 1767 by the Rev. Samuel Locke of Sherborn, Massachusetts, later

president of Harvard. Its builder, Alexander Scott, was a veteran of Rogers Rangers in the French and Indian War, and is reputed to have run Dublin's first public house here. Scott sold to Eli Morse, a weaver from Sherborn. Deacon of Dublin's first church, Morse also built the first gristmill at the outlet of Dublin Lake, as well as the town's first sawmill in 1765. The sawmill ran until about 1886. Morse son's Peter, builder of a Cape cottage nearby, was killed by a rolling log in 1823.

ABOVE: *Davison-James-Bauhan House*
OPPOSITE: *Heald's Tavern*

More conservative, but noteworthy for a doorway complete with sidelights and elliptical fan, is the house that Samuel Davison, a local merchant and drover, erected in 1826 in the Lower Village. The Davison house, like the Morse homestead is one of those Dublin houses so rich in historical personalities and artistic associations that it would be one of the town's shrines even if it were not such a handsome architectural specimen. Such associations, however, should not obscure its quiet elegance and the likely craftsmanship of Rufus Piper and his masonry counterpart, Asa Fisk. Davison was a merchant, farmer, and cattle drover, and his house stands on the site of an earlier 1760 dwelling built by Scotch-Irishman John Alexander. The existing frame ell to the rear is part of a house built here by Joseph Greenwood sometime between 1766 and 1794.[6]

Up the street from Davison's house is Heald's Tavern, an example of the Federal style in Dublin that is of more than local architectural interest.

The 1827 tavern has a clapboard façade and brick end walls, the masonry marked by paired chimneys and shallow full-height recessed arches pierced by windows. The five-bay front boasts a central bay with an elaborately decorated monumental pavilion: the entrance doorway is topped by an elliptical fan, while the windows on the two stories above have smaller fans and are flanked by tiers of triple lights crested with swag-encrusted panels. Because of the richness of this window detailing and the elegant overall proportions, it has been suggested that Heald's tavern was the work of New England's pre-eminent Federal designer, Charles Bulfinch. It seems more likely that Dr. Asa Heald had seen examples of the style in such coastal cities as Portsmouth, Portland, or Salem, not to mention that such details were readily available in builders guidebooks by Asher Benjamin and others.[7] Heald was appointed Dublin postmaster in 1853 by fellow Bowdoin College alumnus Franklin Pierce. Heald's was the town's principal tavern until 1874. The third floor contained a ballroom complete with a spring floor (dismantled in 1900).

Another brick structure of the period was the austere hipped-roof Town Hall constructed in 1823. Dublin's earliest piece of civic architecture, however, was the meetinghouse erected by William Greenwood down in what is now part of the cemetery, opposite the town pound. The town appropriated six hundred dollars to help with the building of the 50-by-38-foot church in 1773. Pew lots were sold to the highest bidders, who were then required to construct their own pews. This crude, rough-boarded building was still incomplete in 1788 when the town issued a warrant "to see what method the town will take to finish the meetinghouse." The article was passed over "to some future meeting" and it is unlikely that the church was ever finished.[8] As early as 1808 the town voted to raze the unheated meetinghouse and erect a new one.

The first meetinghouse was a less than glorious chapter in the story of Dublin architecture, but it is associated with the tenure of the Rev. Edward Sprague who came to Dublin in 1777, succeeding the Rev. Joseph Farrar who resigned as

the town's first minister after only four stormy years in the pulpit. The son of a wealthy Boston physician, Sprague graduated from Harvard in 1770, and, as an eccentric scholar used to the finer things in life, was at first seemingly ill prepared for a pastoral post in a remote agricultural community. Yet this jovial character was one of the town's most beloved figures at his death in 1817 when he was thrown from his carriage.

Sprague enriched the town not only through his ministry but also as a builder. Among the structures he built was the substantial, center-chimney parsonage he erected for himself just west of the Old Common in the 1790s. This square, hipped-roof house still retains its original 12-over-8

Sprague Farm

fenestration while its size bespeaks its owner's considerable wealth. At his death, Sprague left the town $5,000 for the support of the church.

A more suitable meetinghouse was begun with a spectacular three-day raising in June 1818 and it was dedicated that December. Although demolished when its successor was constructed in 1852, the second meetinghouse was clearly Dublin's grandest structure.

The building committee was instructed to make the church "after the plan of Ashby [Massachusetts] or Fitzwilliam." The second meetinghouse was indeed a near duplicate of the example built in Fitzwilliam the year before, which itself was almost identical to that constructed in Templeton, Massachusetts, in 1811. As the builder of the Federated Church in Templeton was Elias Carter, and as he and Samuel Kilburn built both the Fitzwilliam church and the church in Hancock in 1819 (itself a copy of the Dublin church), the second meetinghouse can be attributed to these master builders. Carter is also credited with the Acworth meetinghouse in 1820 and that at Newport three years later, both further variations on the Templeton prototype.[9]

Like its predecessors at Templeton and Fitzwilliam, the second meetinghouse had a shallow portico supported by two pairs of Ionic columns, paired Ionic pilasters at the building's front corners, and a Palladian window at the second-story level. Most striking was the church's steeple that featured a square, open-arched belfry, two octagonal lantern stages, and a short spire topped by a weather vane. This magnificent creation demonstrated that, with the builders' guides of Benjamin or a copy of James Gibbs's 1728 *Book of Architecture*, even a backwater town like Dublin could attain the splendor of the English Baroque, echoing the many churches by Sir Christopher Wren that adorned the skyline of London.

The construction of the magnificent multi-tired second meetinghouse highlighted a period that many residents later fondly recalled as Dublin's Golden Age. Seemingly recov-

ered from the Revolution and the War of 1812, the town was bigger than ever before, and prosperous. Just as the first meetinghouse was associated with the popular and philanthropic Edward Sprague, the lifespan of the new church is indelibly identified with the stewardship of the Rev. Levi Leonard, a man who was arguably the most influential figure in nineteenth-century Dublin.

Like Sprague, Leonard was Harvard trained, but his

Second Meetinghouse

Acworth Meetinghouse

Levi Leonard House

early 1790s, while John Piper was none other than the son-in-law of "Wooden Josh" Greenwood and the brother of Rufus Piper, the town's notable carpenters.

Besides overseeing the library, Leonard managed to find time to write the first *History of Dublin* in 1852, as well as the popular textbooks *The North American Spelling Book* and *A Selection of Reading Lessons for Common Schools*, not to mention compiling *The Christian Hymns*. Not least of Dr. Leonard's many benefactions to his adopted town was that through friendships with many of the intellectual leaders of the day he attracted summer visitors such as the Unitarian divine Theodore Parker to Dublin in the 1840s and 1850s. Due to failing health in the last decade of his life, Dr. Leonard preached less and less, eventually retiring to Exeter, where he died in 1864. His body was brought back to Dublin, to be buried from the third meetinghouse. Former parishioners contributed $600 – a sum equal to that set aside by the town to complete the first church nearly ninety years earlier – to erect a fourteen-foot granite obelisk to mark Leonard's grave in the Dublin cemetery.

One landmark in Leonard's ministry was his conversion to Unitarianism in the 1830s. While most of his congregation remained with him, a group of dissidents broke with the town church and built their own house of worship in 1836, a structure far less elaborate than the second meetinghouse. Simple but dignified, the Trinitarian Church had shallow arched recesses (like those on the end walls of Heald's Tavern) and its two entrances had fans similar to

literary and civic accomplishments were far greater. From his arrival in Dublin in 1820 at the age of thirty, this polymath – he was an etymologist, horticulturist, and musician, as well as cleric – set about to improve the educational and cultural life of his flock. "The Good Dr. Leonard" not only helped found the town high school and the Lyceum, but in 1822 he established the Dublin Juvenile Library, commonly regarded as first free public library in America supported by voluntary contributions. This venture began in a room in Chamberlain's Tavern, but moved into the handsome house that Leonard purchased from John Piper in 1829, just east of the church.

Aaron Appleton built this five-bay frame dwelling in the

those found elsewhere in Dublin. It was demolished in 1877, but it appears in early views as a rectangular box with a square tower; it did not have a steeple, but its crenellated parapets and corner pinnacles gave it a vaguely Gothic revival effect.

The second meetinghouse did not, as might be expected, herald similar structures of equal grandeur in the subsequent Greek Revival period. At a time when the rest of the nation was experiencing the boom of the Jacksonian years, Dublin was declining. From its height of 1260 people in 1820, the population fell to 930 ten years later, and by 1870 – after the secession of Harrisville – it was down to 455. Fertile, easily plowed lands in the west were attracting northern New England youth away from the picturesque but rugged and rocky terrain.[10]

The factories in the river valleys of New England were also luring young people away from upland farms. Neighboring industrial towns like Peterborough, Marlborough, and Keene, and even villages like Walpole and Winchester, have dwellings fronted with Doric and Ionic porticos, but Dublin does not have a single building completely in the Greek Revival – that style associated with the era of Andrew Jackson and America's identification with the birthplace of democracy. This is a direct result of Dublin's lack of water power. Even as an agricultural community, its sheep raising did not approach that in Vermont during this time, where Merino flocks and Greek temples were symbols of wealth.

Instead of recreating the Theseum in white pine, Dublin house builders attempted Greek proportions, usually by placing the gable end to the street, or they grafted details like flat entablatures and pilasters onto earlier buildings. The Gleason farmhouse at the northwest end of Dublin Lake, for example, is a substantial temple-form brick dwelling whose masculine, cubic quality suggests the Greek Revival, but whose detailing is still basically Federal.[11]

Gleason Farmhouse

A more modest example is the 1841 District No. 1 Schoolhouse, constructed two years after the state legislature required all towns to be divided into school districts. Although one of six similar buildings in Dublin, and based upon a standard plan, the simple temple-form rectangle bespeaks the quiet dignity of Greek Revival. The façade is symmetrically divided into five bays of windows and doors – with separate entrances for boys and girls. The school was replaced in 1916 when the district system was abandoned.[12]

Henry C. Piper, a teacher, farmer, and builder, as well as the son of Rufus Piper, built Dublin's most Greek house on Main Street. Here too, there are no great columns or porticos, its only wholly Greek Revival feature is the main doorway, while its construction date of 1854 is later than the most of the temples of upstate New York and the Midwest.

This is the most fully developed of the Dublin houses that turn their gable ends to the street. The corner pilasters are strongly articulated, and the entablature that supports their capitals continues along the sides of the house, while the eaves of the gable throw strong shadows. The unusual second-story window is an individual interpretation of the Palladian window of the earlier Georgian and Federal styles: instead of a rounded central window, it has a pedimented lintel that unifies window and sidelights. The nearly flat lintel of the window is echoed in the entrance doorway. This entranceway is perhaps the most authentic Greek revival detail in Dublin, with its prominent recessed porch. Flanked by a pair of four vertical sidelights and lighted transom

ABOVE: *Henry C. Piper House*
OPPOSITE: *District No. 1 Schoolhouse*

30 above, the entire composition is Greek from its pilasters to its broad entablature.[13]

Dublin lacks the ubiquitous courthouse, town hall, or bank – those temples of commerce and government that were built almost everywhere before the Civil War. Its only monumental mid-nineteenth-century structure is the Unitarian or Community Church, which has dominated the center of the village since its dedication in 1853. (The former meetinghouse site, near the Old Common, was abandoned as being too exposed to winter winds from the lake.) This successor to the churches of 1771 and 1818 employs a Greek temple configuration with a pedimented gable front. But instead of the expected freestanding portico, there is a deeply recessed entrance porch framed by Doric pilasters and a pair of full-height Ionic columns set *in antis*. The church is entered through a pair of doors with heavy lintels, transoms, and sidelights in the Greek manner.

Much of the Community Church's material and some of its architectural details (like the 12-over-12 windows) were recycled from the second meetinghouse. And despite its Greek columns and decidedly un-Georgian feeling, the third meetinghouse is a quite conservative design. The rectangular form and the side fenestration are similar to that used in the eighteenth-century meetinghouse, as was the spire (the present 106-foot steeple replaced the original blown off in the great hurricane of 1938). In part, this reflects the economic climate of the times, but it also bespeaks a commendable caution of local builders empirically continuing

ABOVE: *President Taft at the Community Church*
OPPOSITE: *Dublin Community Church*

earlier traditions to produce a composition that transcended fashion. It is an understated monument that endures as a timeless symbol of the town.[14]

At a time when the rest of the country had abandoned the Greek aesthetic in favor of ideas expounded by Andrew Jackson Downing and other proponents of the Picturesque, and when the Italianate, French-inspired Second Empire style, and all the various Victorian styles were ascendant, Dublin was building plain frame structures. With the exception of the occasional polygonal bay or peaked gable, there is a complete absence of the Italianate or Carpenter's Gothic. Dublin's shaky economy is surely the reason that there are no mansard roofs, that identifying characteristic of the Second Empire, although a number of mansards survive in Peterborough and Keene. One might be surprised to learn that that the front section of the Mason store was built in 1869 or that the Congregational parsonage at the top of the hill was built as late as 1910. On the whole, Dublin's early architecture is, with a few exceptions, unremarkable.

For all its understatement, the architectural heritage of Dublin's early settlement, its 1820s prosperity, and less prosperous pre-Civil War period forms the backdrop for a radically different time when Dublin would reflect contemporary design trends. The discovery of the beauties of Mount Monadnock and the attraction of holiday boarders and later summer residents transformed a sleepy rural hamlet into a colony that would soon command the attention of prominent architects, artists, writers, and political and social figures. Unknown to the celebrants, this watershed can be dated from the Dublin Centennial of 1852 when the town's history as merely another upland village in the shadow of Monadnock closed and a new, more glorious era began.

"Any native of Dublin who returned to the festivities in 1852," wrote town historian Rev. Josiah L. Seward, "found the town looking very much as it had looked for a quarter of

ABOVE LEFT & LEFT: *Dublin Village*
ABOVE: *Mason's General Store*
OPPOSITE: *Dublin from Snow Hill*

a century. The farmhouses were all occupied, herds and flocks were grazing on the hill pastures, teams of heavy oxen were drawing large loads of hay into the barns, schools were in session in the ten districts of the town. . . ." Dublin's population as recorded in 1850 was 1088, almost as large as it had been in 1820, and its cleared acreage outnumbered its unimproved land by a ratio of four to one.

More prescient of the way in which worship of the beauties of nature would change Dublin were remarks by native Daniel Elliott to the centennial gathering. Writing from Marlboro, New York, Elliott wrote of the mountain:

I remember him when clothed with verdant foliage to the very summit. I saw, year after year, the devouring flames climbing his lofty sides, exhibiting him to the surrounding country as a dread volcano or a giant beacon, till half his leafy mantle disappeared. But I liked him best in naked majesty – bald, hoary, stern. . . . I have visited mountains more known to fame – have stood on higher elevations; but from no point have I found the view so satisfactory – uniting so much grandeur, beauty, variety, and extent – as from the brow of old Monadnock. I hail him King of the Mountains![15]

Chapter Two

THE LURE OF THE MOUNTAIN

THERE WAS A minor building boom in Dublin in the 1850s. Most of the construction was to accommodate boarders lured by the mountain and the promise of salubrious air. The Perry-Gowing house on Main Street, built by Captain James Chamberlain in 1773, was enlarged in 1850 and given some slight Greek touches. Farmer Jonathan Townsend added a two-and-a-half-story wing to the 1780 Abel Wilder house.[1]

In 1853, the year after Thoreau's walking trip to Monadnock, the Piper-Proctor house, an 1823 frame dwelling, was enlarged for Solomon Piper. As president of the Freeman's Bank in Boston, timber merchant, and wharf owner, as well as a Dublin native, Piper wanted a suitable house in which to spend his summers. Solomon Piper's younger brother was the carpenter Rufus Piper, so presumably he did the expansion. The temple-form façade features the usual three bays, corner pilaster, and pronounced cornice of the country Greek, but it also has a corner porch, the columns of which have simple ram's-horn-shaped capitals that are no doubt the local builder's interpretation of Greek Ionic capitals.[2] Solomon Piper's house was the first summer residence, but the general building activity was part of the development of Dublin as a summer resort.

In 1846 Hannah Piper Greenwood starting taking in boarders in her house on Main Street, including the tubercular Transcendentalist and Unitarian reformer Theodore Parker who came in 1855. Two years later, Thaddeus Morse opened his house – with its magnificent view of the mountain, access to the lake, and its legendary reputation as Dublin's first tavern – to boarders. The Morses put up guests until Thaddeus's death in 1881. Among their guests were the Isaac Wymans of Brooklyn who came here for their honeymoon in 1867, and the Boston spinsters, Mary Anne Wales and Edith Page, who later built their own summer cottages. In a town without many natural resources, except the view and the health-enhancing mountain air, the lucrative trade of opening their houses to summer visitors was appealing.[3] Another literary giant of the age who came to Dublin in search of the simple life that he said had vanished from Newport, was Thomas Wentworth Higginson. He stayed at a competing boarding house on the lake run by John Mason. He first came in 1879 and eventually built his own cottage on the south side of the lake.

The Grand Monadnock was the draw, of course. At slightly over three thousand feet, it is scarcely grand, but its sleeping lion shape and brooding brow exerted a magical fascination far beyond its relatively modest elevation.[4] Visible from Boston on a clear day, Monadnock loomed large in the consciousness of mid-nineteenth-century writers who were in the forefront of the literary flowering of New England.[5] The mountain fit into the Transcendentalist view of nature as espoused by Ralph Waldo Emerson, Thoreau, and William Ellery Channing. Emerson penned an epic poem called "Monadnoc" in 1847, two years after he first

OPPOSITE: *View of Mount Monadnock and Dublin Lake*

36

ascended the summit. Nathaniel Hawthorne, John Greenleaf Whittier, Oliver Wendell Holmes, and Herman Melville all wrote of the mountain. Melville likened Monadnock to the White Whale's hump.[6]

Monadnock also drew tourists and climbers of the non-literary kind. Thoreau lamented the graffiti carved on boulders at the summit. By the summer of 1859, the editor of the *Peterborough Transcript* noted that nearly a hundred people ascend to the top of the mountain each day. Yet most visitors to Dublin, besides climbing the mountain, came to

read, chat, or play croquet. Perhaps forty boarding houses opened to summer visitors up until about 1880.

For all the bustling summertime activity, little architectural imprint remains. The boarding houses were farmhouses, occasionally spruced up, and those that survived long ago reverted to private dwellings.

Gone too are a few inns and the one large hotel that blossomed during this period. Heald's Tavern on Lower Main Street, long the village's only hostelry (as well as post office), closed down even before Dr. Heald's death in 1874.

In 1871, a Rhode Island physician, Dr. Charles Hazen Leffingwell, came to Dublin and bought the large house on the heights of the village center overlooking the present library, baptizing it Appleton House. Sometimes called Rhode Island House, it became a full-fledged summer hotel through a series of additions. By the 1890s, the Leffingwell Hotel was a rambling, four-story vaguely Stick Style confection of ells, piazzas, and spires, complete with an ornate octagonal gazebo. For all its picturesque gables, balustrades, and latticework, the Leffingwell really fitted no specific Victorian style, nor did it approach in size the mammoth hotels in the White Mountains or along the seacoast. It was really a boarding house expanded to monumental scale. Even so, it attracted a certain kind of clientele that contributed to Dublin's reputation as a place where quiet money could enjoy the mountain air.

The summit of Mount Monadnock in the 1860s

It was probably not un-coincidental that Dr. Leffingwell established his hotel the very year a branch railroad line was opened to Peterborough (from Fitchburg, via Winchendon and Jaffrey). Ironically, the Monadnock Railroad, as it was called, advertised excursions to Newport via Providence. In 1878, the Manchester & Keene Railroad opened up a line to Harrisville, which was connected to the Leffingwell by carriage routes.[7]

A glimpse of the Leffingwell's clientele can be gleaned from the surviving hotel register of 1907–08, when a wide variety of remarkable artistic, literary, and society figures were guests in Dublin. Among the very wealthy were L. L. Lorillard of Newport and W. D. Vanderbilt of New York. The famous clergyman Harry Emerson Fosdick (later the pastor of Riverside Church in New York, but then of Montclair, New Jersey) and his wife were there in July of 1907, as was the sculptor, George Grey Barnard (whose address is listed as New York and Paris), and the author Percy MacKaye, down from the neighboring colony of Cornish. In August, Josiah Quincy, the Mayor of Boston was in residence. Cooler weather brought a Sir Frederick Pollock of London, composers Edward B. Hill of Boston and George Luther Foote of Cambridge, along with architects Charles Cummings and H. S. Browne of Boston, not to mention Ambassador Charles MacVeagh. Frederick Law Olmsted, the landscape architect and parks designer, and the painter Frank Duveneck were at the Leffingwell in 1908. Other names include Clement Houghton, the publisher, Benton MacKaye, the forester and

Leffingwell Hotel

conservationist (there to climb Mount Monadnock, presumably, or to help the efforts to save the mountain from development), painter Martha Silsbee, who would buy a house in Dublin in 1912, as well as Bostonians with the Brahmin names of Saltonstall, Cabot, Coolidge, and Hemenway. New York, Philadelphia, and Providence were also represented.

After the turn of the century, as the building of summer

38

Dr. Leffingwell at the Casino behind his hotel

cottages spread and as the nearby lakeshore became exclusively a private preserve, the hotel's patronage declined, its rooms half empty. On November 22, 1908, Dublin's one grand hotel burned to the ground in a spectacular but mysterious fire, almost taking the village center with it.[8]

Summer prosperity brought smaller hostelries, too. Above the Leffingwell on the east side of Snow Hill, where the slopes were once open to sheep grazing, Professor and Mrs. Richard Burton built a pair of Shingle Style cottages in 1888, known as Boulderstone and Morningside. Burton, a poet and professor at the University of Minnesota and his Baltimore-born wife Agnes Parkhurst, augmented their income by taking in carefully selected boarders. Later they rented Morningside to British diplomat Sir Esmond Ovey and to Senator Medill McCormick of Illinois; his wife was the daughter of Marcus Hanna, the political czar of the Republican Party in the McKinley era. Another grand figure of the latter-day summer colony, Chicago magnate Franklin MacVeagh, later Secretary of the Treasury, rented Morningside in the 1890s before he built his own palatial cottage. The Burton cottages were torn down in the 1930s.

The last enterprise in summer hotel-keeping in this era was the short-lived Willcox's Hotel, built opposite the site of the Leffingwell on the hill overlooking the village center. Frederick Willcox, a South Carolina hotelier, converted Edgewood, Colonel Horace Hamilton's ornate Queen Anne style mansion into a resort hotel that opened in 1910. The business collapsed on the eve of World War I and the house was razed in the 1920s.

Dublin's destiny was not to be a hotel resort. Simply stated, the artists and writers, college professors and clergymen who found Dublin attractive, came in search of a natural setting conducive to contemplation and creativity. These people did not want the ostentatious life of, say Newport, Saratoga Springs, or Lenox, where the virtues and values sought by intellectuals inevitably brought the super rich and those interested primarily in social pursuits or a sporting life.[10]

ABOVE: *Boulderstone*
RIGHT: *Willcox's Hotel*

Lone Tree Hill.   Thaddeus Morse House.   Dr Osgood House   Sunset Hill.   Silas P. Frost House   B. W. Howard House.   Mrs. Copley Greene House.   1 John Sleason House. 2 John H. Mason House 3 Amos B. Howe Sugar Ho

Porch Croroninshield House.   Monadnock Mountain & Lake.   Duble

1880 panoramic photograph from Beech Hill

Handwritten annotations on photograph:
4 Elmer B. Rowe House
Moses A. Brown House
Crowninshield Farm Buildgs.
Walter B. F. Rowe House
V.H. From Beech Hill, 1880

FIVE NEW vacation houses had been built in Dublin by 1879. Fourteen years later there were fifty-six new cottages. Although the early homes did not constitute an architectural revolution, they did set the pattern for what would later be a remarkable collection of architect-designed dwellings toward the end of the century.

An energetic, artistically inclined twenty-six-year-old widow, Mary Abby Mayer Greene, built the first summer house in Dublin in 1872. The second cottage was erected in 1878 by a Boston physician, Dr. Hamilton Osgood, and the third that same year by Mrs. Greene's brother-in-law, a Civil War veteran and civic leader in the Massachusetts capital, General Caspar Crowninshield.

Mary Greene's modest dwelling on Beech Hill no longer stands, but its style and outline are visible in the distance in an 1880 photograph. Solidly conservative, it reflected the traditional vernacular employed in Dublin for decades. With its wide, front-facing gable ends, it was the work of a local builder and not an outside architect and might have been taken for any handsome farmhouse of the period, but for one important difference. It was not sited for practical considerations of New England weather, but rather for its view – a characteristic of almost every Dublin summer cottage built thereafter.

The young widow had considerable impact on Dublin's development by attracting friends and relatives to live nearby. Her recently deceased husband, John Singleton Copley Greene, was the son of an Episcopal minister and the great-grandson of the leading eighteenth-century American painter, while she was related to several old Dublin families. And, when she moved to the south side of the lake in the early 1880s, a number of families followed her.

The second cottage, and the oldest surviving one, was built near Mary Greene's by Dr. Osgood and his wife Margaret Pearmain Osgood, a musician and author.[1] Flint Cottage, a simple frame Greek Revival house is architecturally notable in that it extends that vernacular expression's long tenure in Dublin, for it was only a year later than the second Trinitarian church in the same style. Like Mrs. Greene's summer house and the others that followed, Flint Cottage was intentionally designed as a low-key country retreat, deliberately unlike the grand cottages of the other New England resorts.[2] The cottage is most associated with the sculptor George Grey Barnard, who used it as his studio. Trained at the École des Beaux-Arts, Barnard is best known for his naturalistic portrayals of Abraham Lincoln and allegorical figures (e.g., Two Natures, at the Metropolitan Museum, and Great God Pan at Columbia University). His collection of medieval architectural fragments was purchased by John D. Rockefeller, Jr., and formed the basis of the Cloisters Museum. Like Mary Greene, Barnard discovered Dublin through relatives, for his wife's family, the Monroes, lived next door to Flint Cottage. The Barnards were married on Cathedral Rock on Beech Hill in 1895.[3]

General Crowninshield, like his sister-in-law Mary Greene, not only built a summer residence, but he per-suaded a number of his literary and professional Boston friends to follow him to Dublin. Beech Hill Farm was far more ambitious than Mrs. Greene's cottage on the hillside below. Built in 1878, it was Dublin's first house with indoor bathrooms and a furnace (it also had fifteen fireplaces). Within a few years, the general enlarged the house and gave it a number of turrets, gables, and timber bracing, possibly inspired by the British Executive Commissioners pavilion at the Philadelphia Centennial. This third cottage of the Dublin summer colony was the summer retreat of the poet Amy Lowell from 1901 until her death in 1925.

In 1882 Mary Greene purchased the several-hundred-acre Phillips farm on the south shore of the lake and erected a large house called Skywood. Although extended and enlarged after she erected yet another cottage up the hill in 1900, Skywood typifies the comfortable and relaxed cottages of the period. Not as grand as her brother-in-law's Beech Hill Farm, it is basically a simple frame Dublin farmhouse covered with clapboards and scalloped siding, and featuring a variety of porches that reinforce the informal vacation ambience.

More important than building her own living space, upon Mrs. Greene's removal to the southern shore of Dublin Lake she parceled out land to her friends and relatives. In time, this area came to be called the Latin Quarter because of its concentration of artists, writers, and other kindred spirits.

That same year she built Hill Cottage, a simple frame house that she gave to her friends, Harvard chemistry professor Henry B. Hill and his wife Ellen Shepherd Hill. In one

mer cottage near hers. New York society architects Delano & Aldrich later expanded the Osgoods' 1892 cottage, but we can surmise that when built it was similar to Skywood and Hill Cottage. For Dublin, the emphasis was decidedly on practicality and understatement. Color, such as it was, was provided by the notable literary and artistic guests attracted here and the bohemian life they led.[5]

The fourth of the original Latin Quarter cottages carved out of the Phillips Farm was built in 1883 by Mary Amory Greene, Mrs. Copley Greene's cousin. This too has been enlarged and altered, but it still retains the various projecting bays, porches, cross gables, and variety of surface textures suggesting architectural ambitions greater than the usual Dublin simplicity. The architect was probably the Boston designer, John Hubbard Sturgis, who had partnered with Charles Brigham on two major Victorian Gothic monuments in Boston: the original Museum of Fine Arts at Copley Square and the Church of the Advent, the font of Anglo-Catholicism in New England – and undoubtedly Mary Greene's winter parish – as well as a number of resort cottages.[6]

Far more significant than Mary Amory Greene's choice of architect is that she brought the painter and naturalist Abbott Thayer to Dublin and installed him in the Latin Quarter. Thayer became the most important artist, and surely the most romantic and colorful personality associated with Dublin. Born in Boston in 1849, he studied at both the National Academy of Design in New York and at the École des Beaux-Arts in Paris. Initially interested in depicting

Skywood

of those classic Dublin family connections, Mrs. Hill's sisters, Eliza Shepard Pumpelly and Rebecca Shepard Putnam, were to have an important influence in the Latin Quarter. The Hills' son, composer Edward Burlingame Hill, was chairman of the Music Department at Harvard and occupied the house after the death of his parents.[4]

The Hamilton Osgoods purchased a section of the Phillips Farm from Mrs. Greene and built their second sum-

wildlife, Thayer established himself as a portrait painter upon his return from France in 1879 and became known for his stark and somewhat impressionistic portraits of cultural figures and fellow artists like Mark Twain, Henry James, and Thomas Wilmer Dewing. He was also a great admirer of women, and his paintings of his wife and children, and later women idealized as angels, brought him fame. Thayer also depicted the mountain, and his concern for its welfare led directly to its preservation.[7]

During the summer of 1887 Mary Greene traveled to Keene to attend classes with Thayer. Dismayed by the commute, she offered to build a house and studio for Thayer near

Parker House

her own cottage in the Latin Quarter. So, in 1888, the year he painted Mary Greene's portrait, *Girl in White*, Thayer designed and built a summer cottage that would become his permanent home. That year thus marks the founding of Dublin as an artists colony.[8]

The Dublin summer colony was firmly established in its first decade. The three cottages constructed on Beech Hill and the four on the south shore of the lake were home to a remarkable group of prominent educators and art patrons who, in this short time, had already determined Dublin's future as a retreat for the artistically and literarily creative – and for those who sought their company. The pattern established by Mrs. Copley Greene and her entourage was soon reinforced by the construction of several more cottages.

Richard T. Parker, inheritor of the Boston hotel that bore his name, erected a substantial cottage beyond the northwest corner of the lake in 1882–83. Unlike the Queen Anne or, more particularly, the Shingle Style that would soon dominate the local cottage aesthetic, Parker's house was in a modified Georgian, reminiscent of the work of Boston architect Arthur Little.[9] Eighteenth-century forms provided an increasing part of the Victorian mix, but the chief feature of Parker's house was its broad veranda that gave it an affinity with its more picturesque but informal vacation-oriented neighbors.

Almost simultaneously, Dr. William K. Browne, who, like Parker, was a personal friend of General Crowninshield's, built three cottages on the north shore of the lake. The largest of these, Fairview, was built in 1885–87 in the

Queen Anne Style and features scalloped shingles, oriel windows, veranda, and polygonal turret.[10]

Two other leaders of the Latin Quarter who came in the early 1880s were the bearded, aristocratic Raphael Pumpelly, a renaissance man who combined a career as geologist and explorer with an ardent love of landscape, poetry, and painting, and Thomas Wentworth Higginson, Dublin's premier literary eminence.

Through friendships with Emerson and the Transcendentalists, both men were links to the pre-Civil War era of Monadnock's discovery. Both had abandoned the burgeoning plutocracy of Newport for the simple life of Dublin. As Pumpelly recalled in his autobiography, "We found the Newport climate too relaxing in the summer for the children, and sought a place in the mountains. When we visited at Dublin . . . we found what we craved."[11]

Like Pumpelly, Higginson typified the artists and intellectual summer residents who found in Dublin the solace and inspiration they could not find at Lenox or Stockbridge. A friend of Thoreau and Hawthorne, friend and editor of Emily Dickinson, biographer of Longfellow and Whittier, Higginson was also a Unitarian clergyman, an abolitionist (among the few who advocated violence), a champion of women's rights, and the commander of the 1st South Carolina Volunteers, the first regiment of black soldiers in the Civil War.[12] Higginson built a frame cottage not far from Mary Greene's in 1889–90, called Glimpsewood. Pumpelly's larger and grander Shingle Style house, Auf der Höhe, was built further up the slope of the mountain in 1883–84.

Although not one of the Crowninshield's circle, Bostonian Bartholomew Taggard built a cottage on what was then the undiscovered west side of the lake. Mrs. Taggard was none other than Sarah Piper, daughter of the early Dublin summer boarder and Boston banker, Solomon. Westmere, the Taggards' 1880–81 frame house was a simple version of the Stick Style (characterized by irregular outlines, bracketed eaves, and clapboarded walls). As the local newspaper rhapsodized, "from its numerous balconies, bay windows and broad piazzas the finest view of the lake can be obtained."[13]

Use of the picturesque Stick Style, with its Swiss and

Fairview

Glimpsewood

Westmere

Tyrolean chalets as inspiration, was limited in Dublin, despite its popularity in other resorts.[14] And although the summer cottage boom occurred as the style was waning elsewhere, the emphasis here was mostly on living the simple country life rather than on displays of fashionable rusticity for its own sake. Both Skywood and Mary Amory Greene's cottage might be classified as plain versions of the style. But the best surviving example of that particularly American mode is the Souther-Gleason house, built in 1882 on the site of the first Trinitarian church by Mrs. Freelove Phillips Souther, a member of the family that sold their lakeside farm to Mrs. Copley Greene.

The original color scheme was undoubtedly composed of several hues of brown, but in its present form the house does not look that different from other nineteenth-century farmhouses in Dublin. Yet, the non-structural framing members that articulate the gable end, the brackets supporting the eaves and porch, and the scalloped shingles hint at its former, self-consciously Alpine charm. This early summer residence was pre-fabricated in Maine, shipped to Dublin by train and wagon, and then erected here.

More architecturally ambitious than the Souther house was Colonel E. H. Hamilton's Edgewood, built a year earlier just across the new road to Harrisville. Hamilton was a

Souther-Gleason House

important architect, presumably from a New York firm.[15]

If Edgewood was emblematic of the arrival of a more sophisticated aesthetic than the simpler cottages, the new town hall was an even more visible symbol of Dublin's transformation into an outpost of the Boston intelligentsia. The Town Hall – Dublin's first attributable architect-designed building – was largely conceived and almost wholly financed by the summer colonists.

Dublin, c.1892

local boy made good, although he made his fortune in New York and Mexico rather than Boston. He was seventeen when he enlisted in the First Vermont Cavalry in 1864, so his elevated rank was probably a conceit. A dashing ladies' man, in 1874 he married Hortense Nice, a Mexican girl whose father so disapproved of the match that he sent a gunman to New York to murder her. As Hamilton recalled that his parents had lived in one of Dublin's poorest houses, he was determined to build the best one in town. Given its polychromatic color scheme, abundant gables and bays, terracotta tiles cresting the roof, and Jacobean chimneys, this Queen Anne classic surely was designed by an

48

The Community Church was perfectly adequate for town meetings and civic functions during the somnolent winter months, but it was not suitable for large public meetings or as a place that could accommodate plays, concerts, and the other social gatherings of the burgeoning summer colony. Thus, in 1881 General Crowninshield initiated a campaign for a new town hall by giving $1000; other sum-

Interior of Town Hall

mer residents, including Mrs. Copley Greene, Mary Amory Greene, the Osgoods, and the Taggards, soon donated enough – along with a $3600 appropriation from the town – to ensure the start of construction. A dedication ceremony was held in January of 1883. The architects, Rotch & Tilden of Boston, created what was nothing less than one of the most unusual town halls in northern New England.

Arthur Rotch and George Thomas Tilden both studied at the École des Beaux-Arts in Paris (Rotch had attended M.I.T., while Tilden trained with the major Victorian Gothic firm of Ware & Van Brunt) and formed a partnership in 1880 that lasted until Rotch's death in 1894. While short-lived, the firm designed ecclesiastical, educational, civic, and domestic work throughout the eastern United States, including the town hall in Milton, Massachusetts, the art museum at Wellesley College, and the American Legion Building in Boston.

It was Rotch who actually designed the Dublin Town Hall.[16] As he had just returned from several years of study and travel in Europe and North Africa, the Dublin commission was one of his earliest designs. Young and untested, Rotch no doubt was chosen because of his friendship with the ubiquitous Crowninshield-Green clan. He owned land in Dublin, and in 1884 he built a Stick Style cottage for Miss Emily Sears of Boston, just west of Beech Hill.

The Dublin Town Hall, even in the height of Victorian architectural extravagance, was a dramatic change from the traditional brick or white frame structure in a Colonial or Georgian style. For starters, it had a rich polychromatic color

Dublin Village in winter

scheme, a panoply of earth tones, with accents in purple, red, and green. It also sported a range of textured surfaces, strongly articulated framing members, scalloped shingles, and windows of various sizes – not to mention the bulbous polygonal oriel bays on the sides. Unabashedly picturesque, the Town Hall also had a monumental central pavilion that was quite ecclesiastical in feeling, its spiky shingled spire paying homage to the contemporary Queen Anne style in England, although one might also discover sources in Norwegian stave churches or Buddhist temples. Architectural genealogy aside, the result was a testament to an eclectic free spirit that was particularly Dublin, and wholly American.[17]

The avowed intention of Dublin's early cottages was simplicity. The pioneer cottagers desired a place separate from the world in which to ponder the mountain, read novels, and paint. This remained true for the first decade following Mrs. Copley Greene's settlement on Beech Hill.[18] But with the construction of self-conscious buildings such as the Town Hall and Edgewood, Dublin domestic architecture began to reflect some of the best design of the period. And soon Dublin became a primary setting for that wonderfully exuberant and uniquely American expression, the Shingle Style.

Chapter Four

SHINGLED ARCADIA

IT WAS INEVITABLE that the unprepossessing cottages erected on Beech Hill and along the shores of Dublin Lake would be superseded by more architecturally ambitious structures. The Shingle Style blossomed during the 1880s and New England resorts provided some of the most fertile soil for that inventive hybrid of American Colonial, Victorian, and English Arts & Crafts. Certain Dublin vacation homes would naturally be counted among the leading examples of the fashion.

Just as picturesque in its romantic associations, the Shingle Style was not only a reaction to the skeletal, Swiss-inspired Stick Style, but also represented an attempt to liberate living space. An early Dublin example of the Shingle Style like Professor Pumpelly's 1884 house on Snow Hill conceals the frame behind a thin membrane of shingles. The house, which he called Auf der Höhe – or On the Heights – was also leisurely spread out along the crest of the hill to take in the views and allow for freer, less box-like interior planning. The Shingle Style became an important influence on the development of Modern architecture – notably on the early houses of Frank Lloyd Wright – in that it was designed from the inside out, with the exterior reflecting the flowing living spaces within.[1]

In the wake of Professor Pumpelly's discovery of Snow Hill, with panoramic views both east and west, came other cottagers, among them Mary Ann Wales of Boston. Miss Wales built for herself a large gambrel-roofed and shingled house in the summer of 1886, twenty years after she first began vacationing in Dublin, and her house is a comfortable and unpretentious link to the earlier cottages.

That same appealing and unconstrained approach to domestic design is evident in the large cottage erected in 1888 by two other Boston spinsters, Ellen and Ida Mason. Devoted admirers of Raphael Pumpelly, the sisters had trailed him to Dublin and built their house as close to his as possible (local lore holds that the small arcaded loggia was designed with a view of the road so that the sisters could sit there and watch for their hero to pass by). They employed Alexander Wadsworth Longfellow to build them an

Auf der Höhe

Briar Patch

Misses Mason House

Frothingham and Farnham Cottages seen from Snow Hill

Farnham Cottage

imposing home. Longfellow was the nephew of the poet, Henry Wadsworth Longfellow, as well as the nephew of the Rev. Samuel Longfellow, a Dublin summer resident and a friend of Thomas Wentworth Higginson.[2]

Their summer retreat is notable for the massive boulders on the ground floor, a consciously primitive masonry that echoes the work of the great Romanesque revivalist, Henry Hobson Richardson. Yet, Richardson, for whom the young Longfellow had worked, was also one of the progenitors of the Shingle Style. The shingled second story flares out slightly over the masonry base, but the most prominent feature was a bay over the main entrance rising some two stories to form a picturesque turret.[3] The Misses Mason house joined the Town Hall in the national architectural press when depicted in a drawing in the *American Architect and Building News* for November 30, 1889.[4]

Meanwhile on the northern foot of Beech Hill, two New Yorkers, physician Horace P. Farnham and businessman James Harding Frothingham, erected a pair of spacious Shingle Style cottages in the same year, 1885. Facing each other across the Old Common, they occupy respectively the sites of the 1818 Meetinghouse and the 1823 Dublin Town House. The ridge sits astride the divide between the Connecticut and Merrimack Rivers, and although windblown in winter, it was ideal for summer dwellings designed to take advantage of the western outlook to the lake and the sweeping view down to the village and east across to the Peterborough Hills. All three of the names that have adorned the Farnham house – Breezytop, Far Ranges, and Windswept – testify to the elevated and exposed topography.[5]

The architect of Farnham's whimsical cottage remains unidentified, but whoever he was, he created a handsome complement to the Frothingham cottage. Local builder Willard Pierce constructed both houses, although the Frothingham is more sophisticated. Some of the details are Queen Anne in style, but the unifying brown shingles and the lack of towers on its skyline give this house a more organic and less formal feeling.

The architects of the Frothingham house were Cummings & Sears, designers of that paragon of the Victorian Gothic, New Old South Church on Copley Square in Boston,

Frothingham House

54

completed a decade earlier. Charles Amos Cummings and William Thomas Sears formed a partnership after apprenticeship with James Gridley Bryant, architect of the Cheshire County Courthouse in Keene, and they designed a number of hotels, hospitals, and notable churches.[6] Despite all the shingles, the detailing of the Frothingham house still exhibits some Victorian exuberance. It is not unlike the house described by John Marquand in his 1943 novel *So Little Time*, which was "built in the days when people had learned that you could do all sorts of things with a turning lathe."

With the growing popularity of Dublin among "Proper Bostonians," and the consequent boom in cottage building, it is not surprising that cottagers would discover other areas of town beyond Beech Hill and the Latin Quarter. We've noted Bartholomew Taggard's Westmere, William Browne's Fairview, and Richard Parker's farmhouse at the north end of the lake.[7] And beginning in 1886, the western shore became the setting for an enclave of outstanding Shingle Style dwellings, among them a pair of cottages built that year and the next by Anita Wheelwright, another in Dublin's platoon of Boston spinsters.[8]

The first of these, originally called Banjo Cottage, shares a number of similarities with Mary Wales's house of the same year, namely a gambrel roof and a skin of natural shingles, making it seem almost an integral part of the grove of massive trees that provided its later appellation of Pinehurst. Miss Wheelwright's cousin, the Boston architect, Edmund March Wheelwright, best known for his Harvard Lampoon

Banjo Cottage

building, designed the house.[9] The long veranda and the sleeping porch above it heighten the summertime spirit.

Wheelwright is thus presumably the architect of Miss Wheelwright's second cottage that she built close by the next year for her friend Lucy Bangs. Known locally as Bangs Cottage or Weecote, it was built with a prominent gambrel roof, shingled walls, and broad rear veranda facing Mount Monadnock.[10]

Another of the 1880s legion of Boston maidens was Mary Bradford Foote, the headmistress of a girls' school in Cambridge and guardian of an infant nephew, George. Believing that her two-year-old ward needed Dublin's healthful climate, Miss Foote asked her friend, Henry Vaughan, to design them a summer cottage.[11]

The Thistles

That the Foote cottage, called The Thistles, should have been Shingle Style – with its gambrel roof, broad sheltering veranda, and neo-Georgian details – was hardly out the ordinary in Dublin in 1888. What made it exceptional was that the English-born, reclusive, and self-effacing Vaughan was primarily an ecclesiastical architect, best remembered as the creator of such late Gothic Revival landmarks as the chapels for Groton and St. Paul's Schools, the first design for Washington Cathedral, and numerous Episcopal churches throughout New England. But he was intrigued with the Shingle Style and was certainly familiar with its English antecedents, so Mary Foote's commission gave him the chance to try his hand at New England's current resort fashion. The Thistles retains the tangible Englishness that marked all of the architect's work, but it lacks that self-assuredness, not to mention the horizontal and free-flowing character of the better Shingle Style works.[12]

The grandest and most imposing Shingle Style cottage at the west end of the lake – or anywhere in Dublin for that matter – was the monumental house designed by Boston architects Peabody & Stearns in 1888 for Colonel George Eliot Leighton, a St. Louis financier and railroad magnate.[13]

As a business tycoon and a Midwesterner, Leighton brought a new and not altogether welcome dimension to the quiet, understated Dublin colony of Harvard professors, doctors, and genteel spinsters. The Leightons were in the vanguard of a contingent of wealthy St. Louisans who were to play an increasingly prominent role in the summer colony.[14]

Leighton House

Colonel Leighton's architectural plans, like his aspirations as a country squire on the grand scale, foreshadowed a trend to come. The previous buildings of the summer colony had been relatively inconspicuous, half hidden among the trees and hills, but the Colonel planted his mansion foursquare across an open rise of land where it could hardly escape the notice of every passer-by. And as designers he hired two men who were already famous for such watering-place triumphs as the Pierre Lorillard house in Newport and Kragsyde in Manchester-by-the-Sea, the latter generally regarded as among the classic seaside cottages of the period. Robert Swain Peabody and John Goddard Stearns headed the most successful Boston architectural firm from the death of H. H. Richardson until the First World War.

Monadnock Farms, later called Morelands, was built as a long, three-story cottage, vertically divided by a prominent full-height tower facing the lake. To the north of this turret were the public rooms, the whole surrounded by a wide veranda and sheltered by a broad expanse of shingled roof, broken only by a couple of Richardsonian eyebrow windows. To the southwest were kitchens and servants quarters, topped by a more modest roofline punctuated by a series of dormers. In 1903, two years after the Colonel's death, his son George Bridge Leighton, had Peabody & Stearns make minor additions. Then, in 1916, the younger Leighton extensively remodeled the house, removing the veranda and substituting now more fashionable Georgian revival elements, including a new main doorway with fanlight. His neighbor J. L. Mauran probably carried out these de-Victorianizing renovations. Even with these stylistic changes, Morelands remains impressive. But the original house was, in the words of Peabody's biographer:

> *a fully developed American house . . . its basic rectilinearity and slender proportions in terms of width and length are unusual for Peabody & Stearns at this time, but combine with wraparound porches, wall turrets, gable dormers and staggered steep-pitched roofs to give the building a monumentality of scale it might not otherwise possess. Asymmetrical elevations and rambling horizontality catch the architects and their imaginative and unpredictable best.*[15]

In 1890, Daniel Catlin, another wealthy St. Louisan, as well as George Leighton's friend and brother-in-law, bought the last major parcel of native-owned property on Dublin Lake and gave Peabody & Stearns their second Dublin commission. Catlin, who had made his fortune in tobacco and briefly served as president of Washington University, bought John Mason's farm and boarding house and removed it to make way for his new cottage – thus ending the era of summer boarding houses that had begun thirty-five years before. The Catlin house was, if anything, even grander in concept than the Leighton place, and it marked a new departure for Peabody & Stearns and was a harbinger of stylistic changes in Dublin cottages. Its cost alone – $50,000 – made it the most expensive structure in town.

The 1890s were the firm's best years, and under Peabody's charismatic leadership, they were responsible for more than a thousand commissions. They designed untold commercial and academic buildings across the country and were equally famous for the many summer cottages they designed in such watering places as Newport and Lenox. They were selected as one of the ten firms to oversee and direct the 1893 World's Columbian Exposition in Chicago, where their Machinery Hall was one of the great exercises in the Roman Classical style, forming the Fair's centerpiece and assuring the pre-eminence of the Beaux-Arts aesthetic for several decades.[16]

Seen against this national, even international background, the Catlin house is significant in that it graphically demonstrates the change from the overtly picturesque and non-historical Shingle Style, as we've seen in the designs of

Catlin House

The Thistles, On the Heights, and Peabody's Morelands, to a classical, restrained, and what might be called more "archaeological" Georgian style (Peabody was an advocate of rediscovering American Colonial sources). The house belies its massiveness with an elliptical plan, and despite seventeen gables, a profusion of chimneys, and the employment of a range of shingle and clapboard surfaces, gives an overriding impression of monumentality and elegance. The few vestigial Shingle Style qualities were further subdued by a major remodeling in 1916, perhaps carried out by Mauran.

Peabody & Stearns did not merely design the Catlin house to stand by itself, but as the centerpiece for a large estate whose subsidiary structures, built the following year, reflected the style of the main house. These include a barn (later converted to a painting studio), a gambrel-roofed caretaker's cottage, a stable, and two boathouses. As a utilitarian structure, the barn is less constrained than the big house, with its cupola, wide flaring eaves, and exposed rafters. But the more whimsical boathouses at water's edge added an element of delight to the estate complex, and their folly-like nature epitomizes Dublin's summer colony spirit.

The Catlin house did not mark an abrupt end to the still-vigorous Shingle Style in Dublin, but was rather an indication of the increasing size of summer cottages, as well as a fore-taste of the grander Georgian Revival to come. It also came when new settlements were inevitably appearing in areas away from the lake and the nearby slopes of Beech Hill, Snow Hill, and Monadnock. Boston manufacturer Louis Cabot's 2000-acre agricultural and bird-shooting estate, for example, was situated on Windmill Mill Road. Cabot was the grandson of the Boston mogul Col. Thomas Handasyd Perkins. He served in the Civil War under Caspar Crowninshield, achieving the rank of major, and after a brief attempt at studying architecture, he retired to the life of a country gentlemen. He owned a salmon preserve in Quebec, as well as a quail-shooting compound in North Carolina. When he died in 1914 he was Dublin's largest taxpayer (Daniel Catlin was second).[17]

Cabot did not have to search far for an architect. Edward Clarke Cabot, his older brother, had already designed a summer home at Manchester-by-the-Sea for Louis Cabot's father-in-law, the enormously wealthy clipper ship merchant Augustus Hemenway. Louis and Amy Cabot not only inherited this North Shore house, but also asked Edward to design a summer "farmhouse" in 1887. The result was one

of Dublin's larger Shingle Style cottages, a substantial three-story structure with dark stained surfaces and a massive, blocky outline culminating in two giant brick chimneys, set on a cleared knoll with a view to Monadnock.

Edward Cabot brought to the task almost forty years of architectural experience, beginning with that most Brahmin of institutions, the Boston Athenæum in 1846, and in partnership with another brother, James Elliott Cabot, he

Louis Cabot House

designed scores of notable buildings and estates around Boston. Except for its dark-hued, membrane-like surfaces – these were later painted white, something of an insult to the memory of man who made his fortune in the stain business, the Cabot house bears little resemblance to the staid Italianate lines of the Athenæum of the architect's earliest phase. Yet there is a freedom and unpretentiousness about

Stonehenge

the Dublin cottage that was most appropriate to the summer colony ambience.[18] Even so, Louis Cabot's Dublin house was not conceived as an intimate summer retreat, but as the focal point of an extensive farming initiative – like the Leighton and Catlin places, but on a larger scale – complete with farmhouses, tenant cottages, and a huge barn.

Set higher up on Windmill Hill Road was another Shingle Style cottage known by the evocative name Stonehenge. This was built for artist Martha Parsons of Milton, Massachusetts, daughter of a wealthy Salem merchant, probably about 1889. While the shingle-sheathed upper story and the gambrel roof are not unlike features encountered at Pinehurst and elsewhere, the ground floor and the huge end chimneys are constructed of massive boulders reminiscent of those employed on the Misses Mason house the year before. The Richardsonian eyebrow dormers, suggest – as if such a suggestion were needed – that the architect was a Bostonian.[19]

The Shingle Style was not limited only to the great summer houses. The shingled surfaces, the conscious Arts & Crafts simplicity, and the open floor plans appeared in more modest cottages, as well as in the homes of year-round residents. For example, the small house that Ann Hayden built in 1888 on Church Street below the Town Hall is a simpler version of the Cabot farm. Another cottage that retains the unpretentious but picturesque flavor of the period was that built by Dr. Horace G. Wood at Bond's Corner.[20]

The year 1888 also saw the building of an Episcopal church for the summer residents of a denomination that embraced most of the Boston contingent. Services had been held as early as 1874 and Episcopalians then met in the new Town Hall until their own house of worship was completed. As the building of the Town Hall was realized through the munificence of General Crowninshield, Emmanuel Church was endowed in memory of Mrs. Crowninshield by her cousins Mrs. Copley Greene and Mary Amory Greene.

As might be expected, the architects, Andrews & Jacques, were from Boston. Their rendering of the new church appeared in *The American Architect and Building News* on May 5, 1888. The designer was Robert Day Andrews, a nephew of Robert Peabody. Andrews had studied at M.I.T. and in Europe, and had worked for Richardson. The architect donated his services to Emmanuel, whose building committee consisted of Hamilton Osgood and Raphael Pumpelly.[21]

Emmanuel's first rector, Dr. Reuben Kidner, undoubtedly had some influence on the selection of the architect, as well as on the church's actual design. Kidner's winter pulpit was at Trinity Church on Copley Square, and the plans that Trinity parishioner Andrews donated duplicate (albeit on a much smaller scale) Richardson's open, almost square preaching space of a decade or so earlier. While it follows that Emmanuel does not have the narrow nave and deep chancel associated with the Gothic Revival espoused by Anglo-Catholics, it was skillfully crafted so that the exterior does indeed appear to be cruciform.

The exterior is totally shingled, but it is as much a romantic evocation of an English parish church – with rustic Alpine or Nordic overtones – as an example of the Shingle Style. The church is sheltered beneath a double-pitch roof with prominent overhanging eaves. At the junction of the nave and transepts there is an octagonal, pagoda-like cupola-cum-spire which gives it a vaguely oriental flavor. For almost thirty years, Emmanuel's "steeple" and the Town Hall's original tower carried on a whimsical conversation across the center of the village.

Emmanuel Church

Inside, Emmanuel's exposed timber framing and rich stained glass makes for a felicitous combination of religious mystery and summer cabin in the woods. The windows include a central triptych by the pre-eminent Boston glazier Charles Connick, installed in 1893, and four windows by muralist Frederic Crowninshield, a teacher at the Boston Museum School, Director of the American Academy in Rome, and a friend of Arthur Rotch. Tiffany Studios were responsible for the north transept windows of 1900 and probably for two windows in the south transept installed that same year.[22]

The shingle treatment of the church is echoed in the rectory next door, built by Andrews in 1889. Andrews may also have been responsible for the design of Spruce House in the Latin Quarter (1890), for it is almost identical to the Episcopal parsonage. Spruce House was the third cottage erected by the pioneer Dublin colonists, the Hamilton Osgoods. The steep gambrel roof recalls seventeenth-century New England dwellings and shows the Shingle Style's indebtedness to American vernacular roots, a stylistic dependence that hints at the coming revival of Colonial forms. Spruce Cottage was later the summer home of Josiah Quincy, Mayor of Boston, 1895–99.

Having witnessed the construction of more than fifty summer residences since the advent of Mrs. Greene and General Crowninshield in the early 1870s, Dublin saw the building of only one new cottage between 1893 and 1898. The reason for this was undoubtedly the financial crash of 1893, which affected the moneyed class of visitors. But by 1898, Dublin had embarked upon another building boom. Several Shingle Style houses were erected, but the general style of these more eclectic cottages reflected the national mood, and Dublin too moved away from the casual Victorianism of rustic retreats toward more classically inspired styles.

Though brief, the Shingle Style period in Dublin represents a remarkable architectural achievement. In the choice of architects and in the cottages they built, the town's Shingle Style was equal in quality to those found along the coasts of Maine, Long Island, New Jersey, and Boston's North Shore, as well as the Berkshires. Dublin did not suffer great losses through fire and – thanks to its location – its group of Shingle Style houses remains a notable collection of America's indigenous resort style.[23]

OPPOSITE: *Emmanuel Church, interior*

THE CULTURAL CENTER of Dublin remained in the Latin Quarter. Even more, the area was the haunt of artists, and, as might be expected, its Old World connections were even stronger.[1] The focus of this heightened activity was Loon Point, a compound of houses, studios, and outdoor theatres built by the summer colony's acknowledged leaders, Joseph Lindon Smith and his wife Corinna.

Smith was a painter, Egyptologist, and archaeologist, as well as an amateur actor and producer of plays and pageants. Mrs. Smith was herself an author and champion of the American Indian.[2] The Smiths assumed the mantle of leadership, and together they influenced the direction of the summer colony for almost half a century. Known as Uncle Joe and Aunt Corinna – and sometimes as the king and queen of Dublin – the Smiths epitomized the artistic and intellectual summer residents and Loon Point acted as magnets for many like-minded visitors. Here, they improvised pageants and theatricals, drawing visitors like Mark Twain, Henry Adams, Isabella Stewart Gardner, and Ethel Barrymore, as well as John Singer Sargent, Augustus Saint-Gaudens, and General John J. Pershing – and sometimes enticing them onto the stage. In his plays given at Loon Point, Smith often regaled the children by dressing in the costume of a frog.[3]

Mrs. Copley Greene gave this shorefront property to Joseph Smith's parents in 1889, and with the help of his father, Smith erected a house-cum-studio. During the 1890s he developed formal gardens and also built another studio that he lent to artist friends, including Brush and Frank W.

Benson, the American Impressionist and influential teacher at the School of the Museum of Fine Arts in Boston. The original cottage was later demolished, but the main house, built about four years after the Smiths' marriage in 1899, stood for a century. Framed with a nearly flat hipped roof, Loon Point had a three-story central block framed by two-story wings. It needed only a stucco finish to convince the first-time visitor that it was a country house transplanted from Tuscany. Closer inspection of its various balconies and color accents might lead to a stylistic reappraisal, perhaps something like Italo-Georgian-Frank Lloyd Wright-Chinoiserie.

The house did, in fact, have a forty-by-forty foot summer dining room called the Chinese Porch, which was entered through a moon gate. Boston grande dame and art patron, Isabella Stewart Gardner dedicated the Chinese Porch; she was dressed appropriately as a moon goddess.[4] The porch led out onto a Japanese garden, laid out by Smith in 1905. In its original form, the gardens contained a pagoda, a stone Buddha, and trees given by Japanese statesman Baron Kaneko who stayed with the Smiths following the signing of the Russo-Japanese Peace Treaty in Portsmouth.

Beyond the house was an even more exotic part of Loon Point called Teatro Bambino, a children's theater with an earthen stage defined by semi-circular walls and a stage curtain of trees and shrubs. Additional Mediterranean touches were contributed by Della Robbia bas-reliefs, statuary, and urns, as well a little temple whose columns, reflecting both Smith's practicality and sense of humor, were recycled sewer

66

pipes. Nearby, a similar but larger theater used the lake as a backdrop. Teatro Bambino, built in 1896 with the help of neighbors Higginson and Pumpelly, was purportedly modeled on an outdoor stage in Siena.

In its happy mixture of stylistic sources and decorative elements, Loon Point mirrored Smith's own career as a portrait painter, muralist (he worked with Charles McKim, Gardner protégé John Singer Sargent, and the French painter Pierre Puvis de Chavannes on the decorations of the Boston Public Library), and Egyptologist (he led an annual archaeological expedition to Egypt for the Museum of Fine Arts). Smith also was a successful scout and buyer for patrons like Mrs. Gardner and Charles Freer (whose Washington museum was designed by Charles Platt, architect of several Dublin houses of the period). It is a pity that the houses and studio at Loon Point, along with various boathouses and ancillary structures are gone.

Dublin's character was affected by both the continued arrival of artists like George de Forest Brush and the influx of money from builders of big houses, although many of the old cottagers were still an influence in the old Latin Quarter. Mrs. Copley Greene's last cottage, Lone Tree Hill (rented to Mark Twain in 1905) was joined by her daughter's cottage in 1915. Belle Greene, an eccentric and artistic spinster, extended the early cottage tradition of simple houses designed to take advantage of the views rather than make an architectural statement. Probably her own architect, Belle Greene also dotted the side of the hill with studios that she designed for herself and for congenial artistic friends.

Despite its seeming bucolic isolation, Dublin was more and more part of a trans-Atlantic culture. Even Brush, who was so attached to the town and his farm, felt it necessary to return to Florence almost every winter. The lure of Italy, which attracted so many American and especially Boston painters, sculptors, and writers since the mid-nineteenth century, proved very strong in Dublin. In addition to the whimsical villa created by the Smiths at Loon Point, a number of houses were built around the turn of the century and later displaying both classical allusions as well as more archaeologically correct evocations of the past (they also reflect the fortunes amassed during the pre-income tax era). One example is the 1898 cottage that Miss Susan Upham built for herself overlooking the lake just above the lake club.

Cedar Heights (now called Sky Hill) is severely rectangular and lacks the rambling, flowing plans of some of its Shingle Style contemporaries. Its hipped roof, projecting central pavilion, and symmetrical fenestration seems far more identifiably Georgian, recalling eighteenth-century tidewater Virginia plantations and the aristocratic dwellings of New England coastal capitals. But the front entrance, with its double columns set *in antis* in Palladian fashion, and the pair of pergolas that lead from the west side of the house to what was once a formal garden, are clearly not American Colonial in inspiration (as is, say, the Amory house of the same year).

O P P O S I T E : *Joseph Lindon Smith at Loon Point*

Sky Hill

Tradition holds that this Boston maiden lady's summer retreat was designed by the noted New York architect Charles Adams Platt. This attribution is more than plausible given that Platt was the designer of a similar house built on the north side of the lake in 1900 for Harriet Crownin-

shield Coolidge, daughter of summer colony pioneer Caspar Crowninshield. Mrs. Coolidge's house (now called Mostly Hall, because of the huge entrance hall) shares the same severely rectangular plan, hipped roof, dormers, and tall chimneys, not to mention Tuscan pergolas. This house, too, calls to mind Georgian landmarks like the Wentworth-Gardner house in Portsmouth of 1764. But what sets it apart from earlier American examples is the strong Italian cast created by the recessed arcade across the main façade and pergolas that join the house to the garden.[5]

Platt was responsible for three other Dublin houses. He was just forty when his sister, Mrs. Francis Jencks of Baltimore, asked him to design two houses on Beech Hill. But he already had a decade of experience building houses and laying out gardens for friends and neighbors in the summer colony of nearby Cornish. Remarkably, Platt was trained neither as an architect nor a landscape gardener, although he had studied etching and painting in New York and Paris. He went to Italy in 1892 and two years later published a slender but important volume of essays and photographs entitled *Italian Gardens*. This book, along with Edith Wharton's *Italian Villas and Their Gardens* of 1904, helped spawn a revival of the formal garden in much the same way that the World's Columbia Exposition in Chicago in 1893 had initiated an "American Renaissance" in architecture.[6]

When Platt returned from his Italian idyll, he created gardens for his friends. Understanding the concept of the villa as a dwelling unified with its surroundings, he quite naturally began to design houses that would complement his landscape schemes.[7] Around 1901 he turned to more public projects, becoming known as a campus planner, laying out the grounds for Phillips Andover and Deerfield Academies, as well as both landscapes and buildings for the University of Illinois. He was responsible for the restrained but elegant Beaux-Arts style Freer Gallery on the Mall in Washington and the Coolidge Auditorium at the Library of Congress.

But it was Platt's country estates – invariably designed for very rich tastemakers like Harold and Edith Rockefeller McCormick of Chicago – on which his reputation rests. Sylvania, designed for sometime Dublin summer resident John Jay Chapman in Barrytown, New York, can be favorably compared with the accomplished estates of the pre-eminent English country house designer, Sir Edwin Lutyens. The Dublin houses by Platt are on a much smaller scale, but all speak of quiet elegance, correct proportions, and a sensitivity to their natural surroundings.

Spur House was the first of two houses commissioned by Mrs. Elizabeth Jencks – this one for her sister-in-law and her physician husband, Dr. E. Lindon Mellus of Baltimore. Like the other Dublin houses by Platt, this has a hipped roof, a rectangular plan, and a Doric entrance porch. The rear face of the house originally fronted on a formal terraced garden attached to the house by a pergola. The house is monumental, yet restrained, and totally lacking the unabashedly picturesque elements of Dublin's earlier cottages. In his unerring sense of rightness, Platt did not try to compete with

the house's magnificent setting, with its panoramic views of Monadnock, the Peterborough Hills, and the Green Mountains of Vermont.[8]

Mrs. Jencks's own house, Beech Hill, took its name from the promontory on which it sits, literally straddling the height of land that divides the watersheds of the Connecticut and

Coolidge House

Merrimack Rivers. Designed in 1902–03, it has an even more commanding view than her sister-in-law's house. At an elevation of 1900 feet, it is a prominent landmark visible for miles east of Dublin. Both Beech Hill houses were placed not on the highest spot available, but lower down, where the houses would be more intimately related to the surrounding country. Beech Hill is a far larger house, having a central block and flanking wings. The plan is reminiscent of a Maryland or Virginia five-part Palladian house of the Middle Georgian period (which ultimately had Italian sources). Simple pilasters and a dentil cornice complement the low, hipped roof.[9]

Platt's last Dublin work is the most satisfying of the five houses he built in the summer colony. The Daniel K. Catlin house was erected in 1908 on the site of the summer home built in 1883 by Richard T. Parker. It is adjacent to the house that Peabody & Stearns designed for Catlin's father in 1889. Not surprisingly, the Daniel K. Catlin house has a rectangu-

Aerial view of Beech Hill

lar plan and a hipped roof, but it is different from the other Platt cottages in that it is stucco covered. The west façade features a full-length Doric pergola with flanking porches facing a semicircular garden with central pool. The result is an outstanding example of Platt's ability to integrate house and garden into a single unit and to meld both Georgian and Italian Renaissance elements to produce something uniquely New England. Or, as art critic Royal Cortissoz wrote in his monograph on Platt: "The Italian ideal is so tactfully and with such sincerity adjusted to local conditions that the complete work becomes part of a veritable characteristic American home."[10]

While Dublin could boast a number of notable designs in various styles, the houses of Charles Adams Platt represent the zenith of the classical country house set amidst a formal garden. The secret of Platt's power, as noted by his friend Barry Faulkner, was that the architect understood that he succeeded only when he had educated his client "to desire better and finer things than he had been conscious of before."[11]

One of the most direct links between Dublin and Italy was the painter George de Forest Brush who summered in Dublin and wintered outside Florence, at various rented houses including the Villa il Gioiello in Cutigliano. A number of young painters went there to study and sometimes followed him back to Brush Farm. One such student, Robert Pearmain, had dropped out of Harvard and fled to Europe to study with the great painter of the American Indian and also

Spur House

master of portraits in the guise of madonnas. Pearmain fell in love with Nancy Brush, the eldest of the painter's six daughters, and they were married at Brush Farm in 1909.

Soon thereafter, Pearmain began to build a house and studio on land Mrs. Brush gave the newlyweds and which they called Brushwood. Pearmain died of leukemia in 1912 at the age of 24 and the house was neglected for decades before finally being replaced by "a memorial log cabin" constructed by his widow and her second husband. Reminiscing about

Beech Hill

the place, the former Mrs. Pearmain said, "Robert designed the house himself, studying old Norwegian buildings, as he thought that style would fit in well among the pines." But a photograph taken during construction shows a wonderfully curious wooden structure, with superimposed hipped roofs, a central cupola, and a dramatically peaked entranceway. The putative Nordic cottage place had one very strong Italian Renaissance feature: a loggia of five round-arched windows that runs across the front façade and looks as thought it was borrowed from a Quattrocento painting. Nancy Brush, holding her baby daughter Mary Alice, and looking very much like a Madonna, appears in the central arch.[12]

Another instance of Dublin's own version of the Renaissance is the stuccoed studio and house built around 1913 by Corinna Smith's cousin, the artist Martha Silsbee. This complex on the Old Harrisville Road is another instance of the local tradition of remodeling earlier summer cottages. The Italian-appearing studio was, in fact, added to a frame house built or perhaps rebuilt in 1887 by classical scholar Henry W. Rolfe, professor of Greek at Stanford University and lecturer at Oxford.[13] In 1931 the house, now called Thornehill, was bought by Robb Sagendorph who converted it to year-round use. His wife BeaTrix, a painter and illustrator, took over Silsbee's studio. It was here in 1935 that Dartmouth graduate Sagendorph founded the tremendously suc-

Daniel K. Catlin House

Pearmain Cottage

cessful magazine of New England life, *Yankee*, which, with *The Old Farmer's Almanac*, was published at Thornehill until the growing enterprise was relocated to the center of the village.

The most unusual and intriguing house in the Italian taste was that built by Louise Amory in 1910–11 on her estate off the Old Troy Road. Trinity Hall was a large, three-story, stuccoed composition framed by imposing Italianate towers recalling a late-Medieval fortified town in Tuscany or Umbria. This palatial house and sometime retreat for Trinity Church in Boston was demolished about 1945, save

for the entrance section and a ballroom added in 1926–27.

The surviving entrance front is a 100-foot-long structure with a five-bay, glazed arcade designed by Arthur Little of the Boston resort cottage architects Little & Browne. This evocation of an Italian orangerie is a rather unusual building type for northern New England. Inside, groin vaults span the hall, which has an imposing Renaissance fireplace, as well as a floor paved with decorative tiles from Henry Chapman Mercer's tile works in Bucks County, Pennsylvania. Mrs. Amory became acquainted with Mercer's Moravian tiles when Mrs. Gardner used them in her new house-museum,

Thornehill

74 Fenway Court.[14] The peripatetic Amory had the reputation of constantly hiring and firing architects. Thus, the ballroom that led off this grand loggia was the work of Charles Goodell of the firm of Parsons, Wait & Goodell.[15] Regardless of however many architects this apparently balmy patron employed for her decidedly curious villa, Trinity Hall symbolized Dublin's brief but intense fascination with Italy.

Trinity Hall

The ghosts of Italy at Trinity Hall, the second Catlin house, and Loon Point were further echoed in the studio that the Smiths' friend and kindred spirit, the golden-bearded Raphael Pumpelly erected overlooking the lake on Snow Hill in 1912. Pumpelly's large Shingle Style house, On the Heights, of 1883 was a potential tinderbox, and that teacher, engineer, and explorer wanted a fireproof building in which to store his papers and valuables (such as his notes from the first geological survey of Japan). So he hired Boston architect Walter Atherton, a graduate of M.I.T. and the École des Beaux-Arts, to design a structure with a steel frame, hollow tile walls, and metal-clad windows, all on a concrete slab.[16] The studio is stuccoed, the windows are paired beneath Roman arches, Romanesque capitals are placed atop the entrance porch columns, and various archaeological fragments are embedded in the walls. With the red pantiles on the roof, the effect is quite Italian.

Ironically, Pumpelly's papers were never moved here (and perished when his house burned a few years later), but he did his writing in the studio. Family members used it as a painting atelier and various friends held musical concerts and poetry readings here. The studio's most famous occupant was American dance great Martha Graham who rented it during the summer of 1924.[17]

After Pumpelly's wooden house burned in 1919, he replaced it with an Italian villa, similar in style to the studio. Atherton, a summer resident in Dublin, was nominally the designer, but much of the inspiration came from Pumpelly

Pumpelly Studio

with a walled garden and pool. For half a century Pompelia was a regional landmark. On November 28, 1979, vandals torched the house. Its shell, a lone fireplace with an Italian mantel, and a few exposed beams constitute a sad sentinel presiding over memories of the heyday of the art colony that once flourished on this hill.[18]

Although constructed after the First World War, Pompelia symbolized the end of the summer colony – not only the close of the brightest flowering of Dublin's own Renaissance, but the close of a way of literary, cultural, and social life that did not again rise from the battlefields of Flanders.

Pompelia

and his daughters Elise Cabot and Daisy Smythe, both painters. This monumental two story house had a commanding view of the lake, Vermont, and on clear days the Adirondacks, but it seems more appropriate to the hills above Florence, with its tile roof and stucco walls. U-shaped in plan, Pompelia featured a cloister-like arcaded courtyard

Chapter Six
SUMMER IDYLL

A REGULAR VISITOR described her annual childhood return to Dublin, when the family carriage from the railroad depot in Harrisville arrived at Beech Hill, "coming up the long hill to the longed for, unforgettable sight of Mount Monadnock spread before us, a paradise, where summer seemed to stretch timelessly, a wonderful world without borders."[1] Turn-of-the-century Dublin, like America, recovered from the financial bust of 1893, and entered a happy couple of decades before the "Guns of August" would change the world, and, not least of all, summer resorts, forever.

Dublin's heady natural and cultural climate attracted an increasing number of celebrated visitors, and its vigor was attested to by an outburst of new building. In 1898–99 alone, at least fourteen new large houses were built or were under construction. Modernity arrived, first with the establishment of the Dublin Electric Company and the illumination of two dozen streetlights, and then the first automobile drove into town on September 3, 1900. The State Board of Agriculture's 1905 publication, *New Hampshire Farms for Summer Homes*, substantiated the economic health of the summer colony, contrasting 500 visitors to Dublin in 1890 who spent $10,000 with the 2,000 visitors in 1904 who spent $150,000.

Dublin's transformation in these years reflected the optimism and the nation's prosperity and growth during the McKinley, Roosevelt, and Taft presidencies. Dublin, however, remained a place of refuge for artists and writers. In 1900, for example, Abbott Thayer decided to live in Dublin year round, and his confrère George de Forest Brush bought a house there in 1901. Literary figures of national fame, men like Henry Adams and his brother Brooks, along with critic Irving Babbitt, dramatist Percy MacKaye, and the historian Hendrik Willem van Loon, as well Amy Lowell joined these leading painters.[2] Ethel Barrymore, yet another summer visitor, coached novelist Winston Churchill, author of *Coniston* and Progressive candidate for governor of New Hampshire in 1908, in public speaking.

The most famous personage to rent in Dublin was Mark Twain who came in the summer of 1905 and stayed at Lone Tree Hill, Mrs. Copley Greene's final construction project. Although mourning the loss of his wife, Twain was happy in Dublin, remarking that, "Thayer was right – it is a good place. Any place that is good for an artist in paint is good for an artist in morals and ink. . . . Paint, literature, science, statesmanship, history, professorship, law, morals – they are all represented here."[3] Twain returned the following summer to rent the Upton house off Upper Jaffrey Road.

Lone Tree Hill, or Tiadnock as it was more recently called, has one of the finest views of any house in Dublin. The house has a stretched-out H plan, yet it is only one room deep in the large public spaces and is built along the ridge of the hill to maximize the prospect. The entire north flank of Monadnock rises to the south, leading to a 180-degree panorama that takes in New Hampshire to the Connecticut River, Vermont, Mount Ascutney, and the spine of the Green Mountains beyond; Dublin Lake and more granite hills are visible off to the north.

Because Tiadnock is wrapped in shingles, one might at

. . . . . . and just put my whole heart in it . . . . .

first assume this house is a continuation of the casual cottage style of Mrs. Greene's earlier houses (she purchased the land in 1882 and the house was built in 1900 for her son Henry Copley Greene, author, playwright, and highly decorated World War I relief worker). But underneath the comfortable shingled cloak, the plan is more formal – a long central block that held living rooms, with symmetrical service and smaller sitting room wings at either end. Plus, the house was enlarged following Twain's residency and again, extensively Colonialized in the 1930s. Yet the hipped roofs and pronounced sheltering eaves give a hint of the influence of the Prairie Style of Frank Lloyd Wright – or perhaps it would be more accurate to say that Wright and the builder of Tiadnock both based their work on the English Arts and Crafts movement.

All of these hereditary factors were understood and capitalized upon by Daniel Scully when he renovated the house in 1995. In the spirit of the two noblest country house designers of the last century, Edwin Lutyens and Charles Platt, Scully was able to tie together landscape and house by refiguring garden walls and outlining outdoor spaces with wood gateways and other framing devices. On the long western, scene-facing side, the architect extended, then covered, the open terrace with an open pergola, much in the Platt manner. All these details link inside and outdoors in the best traditions of garden design.

Mark Twain at Mountain View Farm

When George Willis Cooke, minister of the Community Church, wrote, "The absence of fashion may be said to distinguish Dublin as a place of summer residence . . . limiting the summer population to those who have sought in Dublin a natural and recuperative life," he might have been looking backwards.[4] While Dublin did not at first attract the plutocrats who summered in the fashionable watering places, it

Tiadnock

was becoming popular with socially prominent and wealthy captains of industry and commerce. The new class of summer residents was inclined to invite guests for dinner at eight, rather than for supper at six.

Some of these representatives of the Gilded Age included Mrs. Marshall Field, widow of the Chicago department store mogul, who leased both Ty-ny-maes and the Hugh McKittrick house on Snow Hill, while Buffalo philanthropist John Albright rented Mary Amory Greene's Latin Quarter cottage in 1902. Two years later the wildly unconventional financial wizard, Hettie Green – the Witch of Wall Street – rented from Raphael Pumpelly. In 1906, Jane Addams, the pioneer social worker and Nobel Prize winner, stayed in Dublin, and had her portrait painted by Brush. President William Howard Taft visited Dublin briefly twice, once in 1910 and again in 1912.

The influence of well-to-do summer residents was reflected in several large and splendid houses built at the end of the century, such as that erected in 1898–99 by Mrs. Hugh McKittrick on Snow Hill, which demonstrated the national trend toward an architectural eclecticism based on specific historical styles.

A member of Dublin's St. Louis contingent, Mrs. McKittrick commissioned the Boston firm of Shepley, Rutan & Coolidge to build a cottage for her daughter Mary as a wedding present upon her marriage to George D. Markham; she purchased the land along the northern ridge of Monadnock from Raphael Pumpelly. At that time, the land was open – grazing sheep offered just the right bucolic note – and the various Snow Hill cottages were visible from one another. Almost all of the house's nine bedrooms had views of Dublin Lake. It was staffed by half a dozen servants who had even better prospects from the third floor – when they weren't hauling water from the well and heating it for household chores.

The large cottage does have some Shingle Style characteristics – gambrel roof, protective porches, and a comfortable rambling feeling – but it is as much an example of the ascendant Georgian Revival. Here, H. H. Richardson's successors employed classically inspired porch columns, 15-over-15 windows, and other references to America's Anglo-Colonial heritage. St. Louisan George Foster Shepley was the great man's son-in-law, but the house was likely the work of John Lawrence Mauran who headed up the firm's St. Louis branch. The Markham house thus mirrors the movement away from the avowedly rustic architectural expressions of the 1880s to a more historically correct manner; its lines are more formal and the overall ambience is less relaxed than the houses of the previous decade. Instead of extending the life of Richardson's personal Romanesque or his version of the Shingle Style (which was arguably his most original work), Shepley, Rutan & Coolidge seemed intent on directing American architecture toward the Beaux-Arts rendition of Roman classicism popularized by McKim, Mead & White (also products of Richardson's office). The change hinted at less than a decade earlier in Peabody & Stearns's Catlin house appears here full blown.[5]

A western promenade, complete with a fountain, was added to the house around 1910 by the Boston landscape architects Brent & Hall. The massive boulders that form the retaining wall echo – whether intentionally or not – Richardson's stonier-than-stone walls. The most thoroughly Richardsonian detail, however, is the master's signature detail, the whimsical eyebrow window, three of which adorn the top slope of the gambrel on the lake side. The suave and sophisticated Markham house remains one of Dublin's

Markham House

great houses, reflecting the summer idyll at its very best.

This development toward a more Georgian, and hence, ultimately Renaissance, interpretation of the New England summer cottage is even more pronounced in the Shepley office's second Dublin house, begun in 1899 and completed the following year. Knollwood was commissioned by Franklin MacVeagh, a Chicago attorney, grocery magnate, and Taft's Secretary of the Treasury – the president planted two maple trees near the house in 1912. MacVeagh had summered at the Burtons' Boulderstone and then at the Leffingwell, prior to building Knollwood. After a meticulous study of the town, he decided to make his permanent home here.

It was natural that MacVeagh would turn to the Shepley firm. Not only had the architects designed the Chicago Public Library, but also MacVeagh's own house on Lake Shore Drive was built by Richardson, whom MacVeagh no doubt met through either or both of the master's important Windy City clients, J.J. Glessner and Marshall Field. Mrs. MacVeagh – Emily Eames MacVeagh – was very interested in the decorative arts and worked closely with Richardson on the design of the Chicago house. She indubitably worked in concert with Shepley et al. on Knollwood.[6]

Knollwood is covered in shingles, but it is a far more classical and rectilinear composition than the house built for Mrs. McKittrick. The relaxed character of the Queen Anne and Shingle Styles is all but absent in this spread-out two-and-a-half story mansion. The roof is hipped and the fenestration is symmetrical – the whole being rather like a

Tidewater Virginia plantation in rustic dress. The Renaissance sources of the house are further emphasized by the recessed garden, with its central marble basin and pergola (also shingle covered). As one of the town's largest houses, Knollwood is notable more for its size than its architectural finesse. Along with the other grand turn-of-the-century cottages, it symbolizes the transformation of Dublin from an unself-conscious, modest mountainside retreat into a

Knollwood

Knollwood Gardens

more cosmopolitan summer colony. As Marion Whiting recalled in her unpublished memoir, "Irresistible World," the Honorable Franklin MacVeagh "lived in Newport style, surrounded by lawns, terraces, and rose gardens. . . . His extensive house was constantly filled with Washington officials and foreign diplomats for whom he gave elaborate dinner parties, too formal to be very lively. . . ."[7]

Another imposing cottage of 1899 – and one of Dublin's architectural masterpieces – was built by Mr. and Mrs. Edward Frothingham several hundred feet above the north shore of the lake on the western slope of Beech Hill.[8] The architect of Monadnock Hall is unknown, but it was presumably the work of a Bostonian, say, someone like Arthur Little or Edmund Wheelwright, both of whom worked for Peabody & Stearns early in their careers, or, more likely, Shepley and partners.[9]

Later called Holy Wells or High Wells (both names honoring the natural springs on the site), Monadnock Hall is wrapped in shingles, but it lacks the picturesque qualities of Dublin's Shingle Style cottages. It is much less romantic, much more formal. There are two second-story projecting bays, but these are capped by simple gables rather than by medieval excrescences – and they hardly impinge on the smooth, unbroken roofline that emphasizes the house's dominant horizontality. In the unadorned treatment of the shingled surfaces, and in its very simplicity, it appears an evolutionary step between Richardson's Stoughton house of 1882 and Frank Lloyd Wright's Prairie Style. The house was destroyed by fire in 1997.

Monadnock Hall achieved some fame as the summer home of the writer Mariana Griswold van Rensselaer, the biographer of H.H. Richardson. In 1907, the house was the summer home of Count Speck von Sternberg, German Ambassador to the United States.[10]

Another unattributed magnificent house of 1899 was built on Windmill Hill Road and given the evocative Welsh name of Ty-ny-maes. Built by Arthur Jeffrey Parsons, Curator of Prints at the Library of Congress, Ty-ny-maes shared the dominant horizontality and unadorned massing with

Monadnock Hall. Its rough masonry foundation was visible on the downhill side; the first story was clapboarded, while the second story was shingled, as were the attic dormers. This rustic sheathing and the massive brick chimneys recalled the Shingle Style, but the overall rectilinearity of the house – not to mention the tetrastyle Tuscan entrance – gave it a formal character more suited to the emerging Georgian Revival. Later called Five Chimneys (although always known to locals as Tiny May), the house was torn down around 1965.

The late 1890s building surge was not limited to grand

Monadnock Hall

Ty-ny-maes

84

cottages, as a number of earlier Dublin houses and cottages were enlarged or remodeled. On Parsons Road, not far from Ty-ny-maes, a farmhouse built in 1816 by school agent Moses Corey was extensively made over around 1895 as a summer residence by Georgiana Parsons, a wealthy amateur artist. This early Cape, enlarged with a variety of porches, peaked gables, and dormers that contribute a lively skyline, took on the rambling look of an English country cottage.[11]

The William Wymans enlarged an eighteenth-century farmhouse on Old County Road, originally erected by Revolutionary war veteran William Strongman, during that bumper year of 1899. The Wymans, who lived in Brooklyn in the winter and had been coming to Dublin since their honeymoon in 1867, attempted a recreation of a seventeenth-century New England dwelling, such as the 1683 Parson Capen house in Topsfield, Massachusetts.[12] The seventeenth-century proportions of the Wyman house were unusual, for most of the turn-of-the-century homes relied upon eighteenth-century models – the interest in recapturing our Colonial architectural heritage may be said to have begun with a walking tour of New England undertaken by Charles McKim, William Rutherford Mead, and Stanford White in 1878.

A house in full Colonial Revival dress is that built by William Amory, one of New Hampshire's wealthiest men, in 1898-99 off the Old Troy Road. Amory was a Bostonian, as was his designer, John Lavalle. Although one of the least remembered of Dublin's architects, the Peruvian-born,

M.I.T.-trained Lavalle was an extremely well connected and much-in-demand country house designer. In addition to being responsible for the Massachusetts Building at the Jamestown Exposition of 1907, Lavalle did three cottages on the fashionable Maine resort island of Islesboro at the same time as the Amory house, as well as seaside homes for the very rich from Cohasset to Beverly Farms.[13]

The Amory house competently employs elliptical bays, Roman bath windows, Tuscan porch columns, and the all-white color scheme of the neo-Colonial style. Given the busy state of Lavalle's office as it provided country estates for well-to-do Bostonians, the Amory house is expectedly quite similar to an Islesboro house of the same year – so much so that a historian's description of the Dr. George Shattuck cottage in Maine could have been written about the Amory house. Both summer cottages feature the distinctive swooping bell-cast Dutch Colonial roof. What John Lavalle "created for his client was a free interpretation of a two-and-a-half story New England gambrel roofed house of the eighteenth century. . . . Such exaggerated features as wide clapboards and multi-paned sash characterize this cottage as a playful rather than an academically correct reflection of the period."[14]

Not surprisingly for a summer colony that attracted writers and intellectuals like Mark Twain and Henry Adams, university professors continued to play a prominent role in determining the tone of the colony and to have an effect on its architectural design. The largest academic delegation by far was from Harvard, including Pumpelly (that school's first

ABOVE: *Amory House*
RIGHT: *Mrs. Amory*

86

professor of mining), chemist and Nobel laureate Theodore W. Richards,[15] and historians Albert Bushnell Hart and Ernest Henderson.[16] "The reasons for making a summer place in New Hampshire," Hart wrote in *New Hampshire Farms for Summer Homes*, a state-sponsored publication that encouraged development, "are very simple: We were attracted by the delightful air, by the superb near and far views, by the excellent and romantic roads, by the walks and mountain climbing, and the general opportunities for outdoor life. We were especially drawn to Dublin by the good neighbors."[17] Hart, best known for his historical treatise *The American Nation*, constructed a large Shingle Style house in 1899–1900 on a hill above the village. An amateur architect, Hart most certainly designed Hill House, which, with its gambrel roof and wide veranda, is more like the cottages of the 1880s. It also featured a ballroom where Hart delivered lectures.

Albert Hart's neighbor, William Brooks Cabot, an explorer, as well as the brother of Louis and Charles Cabot, built a substantial cottage in 1905 closer to the center of the village. Despite a sheathing of shingles, all references to the frivolity of the Shingle Style were replaced by classical fenestration and details. The British Embassy staff, including Lord Eustace Percy, son of the Duke of Northumberland, was housed here during the summer of 1910.

A non-Harvard professor, John Osborne Sumner, an architectural historian at M.I.T., built a large, two-and-a-half story house called Road's End shortly after his marriage in 1900. The white clapboard Colonial Revival home combines eighteenth-century details under a broad roof with bracketed eaves that gives an air of reposeful elegance that is unmistakably turn of the century, while its sense of comfort taking precedence over pure aesthetics is very Dublin. The house has been greatly modified over the years.

Many of these new cottages had views of Mount Monadnock, but none of them was on the shore of Dublin Lake, as much of the shoreline had been appropriated by the earlier cottagers. Thus, the Dublin Lake Club was founded in 1901 to provide bathhouses, tennis courts, and a sailing

Road's End

wharf, but also a clubhouse to serve as a social center for Dublin's summer colony.[18]

The clubhouse, which opened on August 19, 1902, is a single-story, hipped-roof structure covered with rough boards; it has a broad veranda supported by rough-hewn columns on its north and west sides. The architecture of the Lake Club – a collaborative effort by Joseph Lindon Smith and his wife Corinna, and no doubt with the assistance of John Lawrence Mauran and maybe other talented club members – is a relaxed mixture of remembered styles and mountain resort rusticity. The club featured literary gatherings and amateur theatricals, bringing in the talents of guests like Twain, Lowell, and Henry Adams; conventional country club fare – liquor, meals, and parties – was not allowed.

Following construction of the Lake Club, a number of summer residents erected half a dozen boathouses along the shore on either side of the club beach, mostly between 1901 and 1920. The most ambitious of these is the two-story, half-timbered and shingled boathouse, long owned by Aimée Lamb, Arthur Rotch's niece. Collectively, the boathouses, like those built by Peabody & Stearns for the Catlins, along with that designed by Mauran at Homewood on the west side of the lake, remain enduring symbols of Dublin's summer colony and its love affair with the lake.

ABOVE RIGHT: *Lake Club*
RIGHT: *Lamb Boathouse*

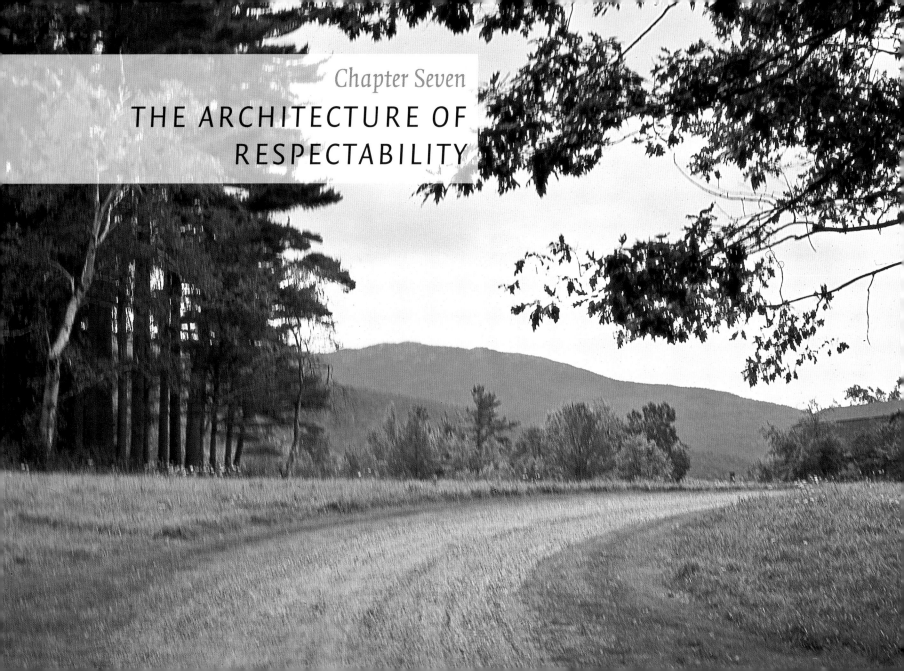

Chapter Seven

THE ARCHITECTURE OF
RESPECTABILITY

DESPITE THE obvious appeal of the houses erected during Dublin's love affair with Italy, these bountiful years in the life of the art colony witnessed the construction of cottages and public buildings in a variety of other styles. An often joyous borrowing and creative re-interpretations of different historical styles characterized American architecture of the period from the Gilded Age to the Great Depression.

The Georgian and its American Colonial derivative were ultimately based on the Renaissance, but these classical styles were challenged by the remembrance of the architecture of the Middle Ages. The Romanesque, for example, which so inspired Richardson and his followers, and also the Gothic, which had been popular in the mid-nineteenth century, were undergoing a vigorous revival (led in part by Henry Vaughan, the designer of The Thistles), particularly for churches and academic buildings. The picturesque details, massing, and spirit of medieval styles had infused the Dublin cottages of the Victorian period. Still, the Renaissance aesthetic fostered by the Beaux-Arts classicism of the Chicago World's Fair of 1893 – and including the Georgian and Colonial – pretty much dominated the Dublin architectural scene.

Also, the building of new summer cottages was augmented by the local tradition of altering and stylistically updating earlier houses. One example of extensive remodeling was the old Nathan Bixby farm off Upper Jaffrey Road that was undertaken in 1903 by John Lawrence Mauran, a St. Louis architect who summered in Dublin. The work was commissioned by George and Alice Upton of Boston, who bought the house in 1885 and wanted it remodeled for summer use. To the front of this 1780s farmhouse, Mauran added a two-and-a-half story, six-bay Georgian Revival façade, featuring heavily dentiled cornices, a long colonnaded veranda, and Palladian windows. Mountain View Farm, so named because of its spectacular prospect of the eastern slope of Monadnock and the Massachusetts hills, is a textbook illustration of the transformation of Dublin's early settlement mode into the Colonial Revival of the early twentieth century.

89

Mountain View Farm

Its larger scale and richer detailing bespeaks the wealth and architectural pretensions of the summer colonists.

The house's real importance lies in the fact that Mark Twain rented it in 1906, the second of two summers spent in Dublin. Twain claimed he had been too distracted in "Little Bohemia" near the lake and so he relocated two miles from the village in the "scientific quarter," so called because of the area's popularity with businessmen and scientists. Twain's biographer, Albert Paine Bigelow, wrote of the farm: "It stands at the edge of a beautiful beech forest, just under Monadnock . . . overlooking one of the most beautiful landscape visions on the planet; lake, forest, hill, and a far range of blue mountains. . . . I have seen these things in paintings, but I had not dreamed that such a view really existed." Despite the personal shadows that hung over Twain's two summers on the slopes of Mount Monadnock, he summed up his affection for Dublin, calling it "the one place I have always longed for, but never knew existed in fact until now."[1]

John Lawrence Mauran had a significant impact on Dublin architecture of the period, in fact more so than any other designer including Charles Platt. Born in Providence, Rhode Island, in 1866, he was a graduate of M.I.T. and also studied in Europe.[2] Returning to the United States in 1892, he entered the Boston office of Shepley, Rutan & Coolidge, designers of Knollwood and the McKittrick house. He was soon transferred to Chicago to supervise the construction of the Chicago Public Library and the Chicago Art Institute, and thence to St. Louis to establish yet another branch of the ven-

John Lawrence Mauran

erable firm. It was there that he met Isabel Chapman, whose parents summered in Dublin.[3]

Mauran's career reflected the architectural changes of the period – note the change in Shepley, Rutan's work from a medieval-inspired Victorian to more classical Roman, Renaissance, and Georgian styles. In 1900, Mauran established his own firm in St. Louis, by which time his reputation was more than secure. He was a member of the MacMillan Commission set up by Congress (and headed by Charles McKim) to oversee the beautification of Washington along the lines of Pierre Charles L'Enfant's original plan, and in 1906 he was the United States delegate to the Sixth International Congress of Architects in Madrid. President Theodore Roosevelt appointed Mauran to the powerful Fine Arts Commission in 1908, the same year the architect served as a presidential elector – he supported future Dublin summer visitor William Howard Taft. The pinnacle of Mauran's professional achievement came with his election to the presidency of the American Institute of Architects in 1915, a post he held for three years.

A more public design than the second Twain house was Mauran's remodeling of the Dublin Town Hall in 1916. The entire front spire was removed and in its place the main gable received a monumental Palladian window, and the building was painted white. Mauran presumably had no hesitation about eradicating the "Hansel and Gretel Gothic" of Arthur Rotch's first work. Apparently no one in the village expressed any regret at losing an exuberant and bold High Victorian landmark and getting in its place a rather pedes-

Remodeled Town Hall

trian façade (although it might be noted that Mauran did the Town Hall renovation gratis and paid for the burying of telephone wires in the center of town as well).

Two years later, perhaps drawing upon his grander experience in civic planning with the MacMillan Commission,

Mauran designed the oval in the center of Main Street, between the Town Hall and the General Store. A gift from Mrs. Mauran in memory of her parents, the little, granite-fringed greensward was part of the construction of the South Side Highway of 1914–18 that came through Dublin along Main Street. As a further instance of civic betterment, the Village Improvement Society, of which Mauran was a leading member, buried utility wires underground.[4]

In 1916, while remodeling the Town Hall, Mauran designed another municipal building, the Dublin Consoli-

Dublin Oval

dated School. Farther down Main Street toward the Lower Village and Peterborough, and next to the 1841 District No. 1 Schoolhouse that it replaced, Mauran's composition is a handsome and restrained exercise in the Georgian style. Built of brick, the new school is a single monumental story on a raised basement in Palladian fashion, lighted by large, multi-paned windows. The most prominent Georgian feature is the front entrance, boasting a semicircular fanlight, pilasters, and pediment.

The Town Hall facelift, the school, and the village oval are the last works that Mauran executed in Dublin and their uncompromising formality suggests the St. Louis architect had always been a classicist. Buildings with sources in the Middle Ages, however, continued to exert an influence here, and one of Mauran's first Dublin projects appeared in more medieval garb.[5]

Dublin's other major public structure, the Town Library, was also by Mauran. Built in 1900–01, the library shows the architect as a not inconsiderable Gothic Revivalist. Housing the successor to Dr. Leonard's Dublin Juvenile Library, the new library is constructed of massive boulders from Maine and sheltered by a broad slate roof. Despite the Gothic feeling imparted by the Tudor bargeboards framing the entrance and the half-timbering on the gables, the plan derives directly from the iconic small-town libraries of H.H. Richardson – predecessor of Mauran's former teachers and employers, Shepley, Rutan & Coolidge.

Like Richardson's Romanesque libraries in the Boston

Dublin Consolidated School

Dublin Pubic Library

suburbs of Quincy, North Easton, and Woburn, the Dublin composition is divided into three major and clearly articulated sections. There is an entrance and administration area, a reading room to the west, and the large stack area to other side of the entrance hall. The interior has massive exposed beams and was heated by three huge fireplaces – another recollection of Richardson from the 1870s and '80s.[6]

Mauran's earliest domestic design in Dublin was the large cottage he built on Snow Hill for Thomas H. McKittrick of St. Louis in 1900.[7] The house featured a rubble masonry base, shingled walls, and a series of peaked gables – recalling the neighboring Misses Mason house and pre-figuring Mau-

ran's most important Dublin work, Homewood. Snow Hill, as the house was called, was colonialized in 1914 by Washington architect Nathan C. Wyeth. The house suffered the same fate as Pompelia, when it was burned by vandals in 1978.[8]

Like Snow Hill, Mauran's domestic masterpiece is also gone. Homewood was built for Mauran's mother-in-law, Mrs. J.G. Chapman, on a commanding site on the west side of the lake. Anita Wheelwright's Banjo Cottage – then Mauran's summer home – was moved to make way for the new house. Constructed at the same time as the town library, Homewood is a significant example of the architect's work before his complete conversion to neoclassicism. The new

Snow Hill

Snow Hill, Wyeth renovation

cottage was constructed of shingle, timber, and brick, and its large, rambling, two-and-a half-story configuration, combined Shingle Style and Tudor motifs – porches, Gothic bargeboards, half-timbering with brick infill, polygonal bays, and turreted staircases. Despite these English Arts & Crafts details, the plan was essentially classical; the main façade was symmetrical and the two projecting Tudor wings were connected by an arcade – a form not unlike that employed by Charles Platt at the Daniel K. Catlin house.[9]

One could imagine, perhaps, Homewood perched ex-

posed on the seaside cliffs at Newport, but much of its magic lay in its landscaping. Mauran most certainly designed the terrace facing Monadnock and the small garden to the west. Brick walls on three sides framed the rectangular perennial garden and there was a central grass oval accented by a sundial, gravel paths, and formal hedged beds. There was a summer house, and a lion's-head fountain with a basin adorned the curved north parapet. An opening on the south led to a brick-paved giardino segreto, enclosed by euonymus, yew, and hemlock, as well as larger specimen trees that framed the view of Monadnock. Mrs. Mauran used the gardens as the subject for her bookplate.

Mauran also designed Ethan Allen Hitchcock's house, built in 1901–02 on the west shore of the lake, north of Homewood. Hitchcock recalled his first visit to Dublin when he was "so struck with the superb views to be had in all directions of old Monadnock, the delightful drives, the delicious air, and quiet restfulness of its surroundings" that he rented "what was then known as the Taggart cottage." Hitchcock purchased Bartholomew Taggart's Westmere in 1896, but decided he wanted a far grander "cottage of colonial design."[10] It was a large, two-story white frame structure combining elements of the architect's medieval past and Georgian future. The Richardsonian eyebrow dormers on the front roof and the full-height stair tower-turret on the rear harked back to Mauran's Shepley-inspired work, while the Tuscan columns supporting the front porch and the Palladian entrance were more formal. Hitchcock, Secretary of the Interior under McKinley and Theodore Roosevelt, named his new place after the old one, and it was at Westmere that he found it easier "to play Cincinnatus with the stage settings that surrounded him than to prosecute the timber thieves, the land fencers and the cattlemen of the West."[11]

Lawrie Mauran, beyond his architectural legacy, was an important and beloved figure in the summer colony. Handsome and dapper, he was also a devoted family man who threw himself into the house parties and amateur theatricals that characterized Dublin in these years.[12]

Homewood

Isabel Mauran's bookplate

Hitchcock House

Catholic Church, "My Lady of the Snows", Dublin, N. H.

Our Lady of the Snows

Just as Mauran's school and made-over Town Hall, along with the Community Church, form a triumvirate of classical architecture in the center of Dublin, the library, Emmanuel Church, and Our Lady of the Snows Church form a triad of medieval public buildings. Though they were erected a decade and a half apart, both churches were built by important ecclesiastical architects from Boston and were intended to serve as summer parishes. Like Emmanuel, the newer church rated an illustration in *The American Architect and Building News*.

Our Lady of the Snows (which despite its appellation, was used solely in the summer) was built in 1904 to the designs of Frank A. Bourne. A graduate of M.I.T., Bourne worked for the ubiquitous Shepley, Rutan & Coolidge before establishing his own practice, which specialized in domestic and ecclesiastical work. He designed several Episcopal and Congregational churches across New England, as well as approximately seventy houses in Boston's Back Bay; he was the author of *A Study of the Orders of Architecture* (1906). What was unusual about this Roman Catholic house of worship was that it was commissioned and paid for by several prominent residents – Thomas Wentworth Higginson, Louis Cabot, Daniel Catlin, Franklin MacVeagh, and George Leighton – none of whom was Catholic. Our Lady was built for the servants of the summer people who themselves worshipped at Emmanuel or the Unitarian Church.

Our Lady is Gothic Revival, but it also incorporates something of the feeling of the Shingle Style vacation cottages. Unlike Emmanuel, Our Lady's plan was more liturgically traditional, consisting of a rectangular nave divided into four bays terminating in a polygonal apse. The church is shingled and has a steeply pitched roof with pronounced eaves. There are three peaked dormers on each side of the roof and an octagonal cupola with cross over the first bay. The strongest – and most English – element is the massive entrance porch, the timbers of which echo those that span the interior. A handsome country parish church – more Anglo-Catholic than Roman Catholic, however – Our Lady recalls similar ecclesiastical works by Henry Vaughan and Rotch & Tilden.[13]

The Dublin summer colony's most overtly medieval house carried the evocative Scottish name of Fasnacloich. It was built in 1911 (and enlarged in 1916-18) by Charles and Fanny Davenport Rogers MacVeagh, just over the line in Harrisville. The architect of record was a New Yorker, Alexander Ball, although Mrs. MacVeagh undoubtedly had much to say about the design. Charles MacVeagh was the nephew of Franklin MacVeagh of Knollwood, while Mrs. MacVeagh was the author of *Fountains of Papal Rome* (1915). Their house is an idiosyncratic but convincing blend of Elizabethan and Jacobean styles – a Cotswold manor house seemingly imported from Gloucestershire. Fasnacloich is set amid an Elizabethan garden, which, like that at Homewood, frames a dramatic view of the Monadnock.

Fasnacloich

If the picturesque inspired these few houses and churches, the Georgian and its Colonial cousin were still the favorites for the smaller houses built by some of Dublin's six hundred year-round citizens. For example, the 1905 gambrel-roofed dwelling on Church Street built for James Porter is Colonial Revival, as is the frame 1911 Alfred Greenwood house across the street.[14] Porter's builder, James L. Brockway, was a Canadian immigrant, as was Greenwood (a housepainter who anglicized his name from Boisvert), and they were among the new settlers of Irish, Italian, Finnish, and French-Canadian extraction who broadened and enriched Dublin's hitherto almost exclusively Yankee and Scotch-Irish stock. Although a relatively small element in rural Dublin compared to their numbers in nearby manufacturing towns, these newcomers – especially the Finns, who took up small-scale farming – and their descendants were to play an increasingly substantial role in community life.

Leaven though these newcomers were to the Dublin loaf, it was not their modest dwellings but the largest cottages built by the summer residents that are the important protagonists in the town's architectural story. In addition to the Italian villas, the houses of Mauran, and the new church, there were yet other significant houses, most displaying the classical elegance of the Georgian, erected here before the Great War.

One such large house was Fairwood, designed by the Boston commercial and hospital architects Densmore, Le Clear & Robinson in 1910 for Mrs. Charles F. Aldrich. She constructed her new house around the 1855 Silas Frost farmstead that was totally obscured by the profusion of new wings, dormers, pediments, and bay windows. Fairwood was the summer home of the pioneer aviator and Antarctic explorer, Admiral Richard E. Byrd, who lived here for the seasons of 1930 and 1931.[15]

A year after construction of Fairwood there was another enlargement in the Georgian style, not of an early farmhouse, but of Dr. Hamilton Osgood's 1882 Latin Quarter cottage on the south side of the lake. Following Osgood's death in 1907, the family sold the cottage, which was all but swallowed up by new additions. A somewhat picturesque skyline formed by a variety of chimneys, gables, and dormers remains; Highfield's monumental and imposing quality

reflects the imprint of Delano & Aldrich. The New York firm ranked among the country's premier Georgian Revival practitioners and was known for its elegant townhouses and country estates for the very rich.[16] The house – later called Beaglesmere – was further remodeled in 1964 by Boston architect James Hopkins, whose father was a principal with the distinguished Georgian and later Modernist firm of Kilham & Hopkins.

Walter Kilham and James Hopkins, noted for designing of the *Atlantic Monthly* headquarters in Boston and several buildings at Radcliffe College, also were responsible for the last pre-World War I summer house in Dublin.[17] Rather than stressing comfort over aesthetic statement, Kilham & Hop-

Fairwood

kins's design for fellow Bostonian Harry Seaton Rand on the Old Harrisville Road is one of the most academic Georgian compositions in Dublin. Built in 1917, this brick house, with its elongated curving plan, and variably sloped roofline, is, in keeping with the historically accurate classicism of the early twentieth century, more English in flavor than American.[18]

Arguably the finest example of the neo-Georgian associated with the Dublin summer colony is Skyfield, built in 1916 just up the road from the Rand place. It replaced Arthur Rotch's 1894 summer cottage, which had burned two years earlier. This graceful rendition of the English country houses of the Restoration period calls to mind the work of Sir Christopher Wren, themselves sources for American Georgian. Skyfield is a major work of Lois Howe, principal of the first all-woman architectural firm in the United States, and it demonstrates the architect's knowledge of early American architecture and its sources.[19] One of Dublin's largest cottages, Skyfield jettisoned easy informality for a quiet, symmetrical probity. The plan forms an elongated H, with two flanking hipped roof wings and four tall chimneys. Unusual for Dublin, too, is that the house sits on a large open field with a commanding view of the mountain.

That pioneering female design firm was probably responsible for a more modest, yet equally assured neo-Colonial house just above Stone Pond at the very western edge of Dublin built in 1932. This was the summer home of the writer Eugenia Brooks Frothingham, a long time vacationer whose parents had built High Wells at the turn of the

Skyfield

High Meadows

marks of Lois Lilley Howe's work, and while no documentation has surfaced to definitely ascribe the house to Howe, the ever-popular lady architect did design the ever-popular lady writer's winter home in Cambridge in 1922.[20]

Called by the evocative name High Meadows, this tallish and comfortable frame house is marked by a plan that bends the house near the middle, so that it forms a welcoming courtyard on the entrance side. The other side thus wraps around more of the meadow's crest and offers an extended view of lake and mountain, recalling the sun-trap plans of the English twentieth-century master of the country house, Edwin Lutyens. The clapboards, shuttered six-over-six windows, and colonnaded sun porch all contribute to a gracious yet almost suburban composition. The glimpse of Monadnock between the house and the formal garden recalls the appearance of a volcano – Vesuvius or Etna, perhaps – seen across the *campagna*.

Less grand – that is, more Colonial than English Wrenaissance – but one of the largest houses built in Dublin before the war, was the farm constructed on Windmill Hill Road in 1909–10 by Arthur Jeffrey Parsons. Dayspring was near the end of a group of substantial summer cottages erected by members of the Parsons family, beginning with Stonehenge in 1888.[21]

Local tradition holds that the Parsons farm was the model for the Dublin estate of "old Mrs. Forbes," the Boston matriarchal grande dame of Frances Parkinson Keyes's 1950 novel *Joy Street*. Like other cultured and wealthy Bostonians

century. Author of numerous novels, most of which make reference to summer life at the base of the mountain, Frothingham was pulled to Stone Pond by her friendship with Justine Houghton Kershaw, matron of the big house on the pond, Merrywood. The Frothingham house has all the hall-

before her (we feel sure that she was part of the Crownin-shield-Copley Greene-Church of the Advent circle), Mrs. Forbes disliked Newport and Cape Cod. She owned a house at Manchester-by-the-Sea (undoubtedly designed by Arthur Little or Robert Swain Peabody), but she regarded her Dublin farm as a non-social and recuperative retreat.[22]

Dayspring marked a close to the story of Dublin's pre-World War I days. The house burned to the ground in 1982.[23]

Dayspring

Chapter Eight

THE SUMMER COLONY
REMEMBERED

THE RANGE AND brilliance of the pre-World War I summer colony were never matched after 1918. Thomas Wentworth Higginson died in 1911, Abbott Thayer in 1921, Raphael Pumpelly two years later, and Amy Lowell in 1925. Luminaries of the stature of Mark Twain or Henry Adams no longer sought houses for the summer season. Nevertheless, Dublin's strong cultural traditions survived the war, the income tax, and the Great Depression. And while the finest flowering of Dublin as an artists colony had passed, the community on the slopes of Mount Monadnock still attracted important culturati.

The flavor of early twentieth-century Dublin was captured by Marion Schlesinger Whiting, who with her inventor husband Jasper, began to summer here in 1919. They remained seasonal visitors until 1927 when they bought a house on Old Harrisville Road and stayed year round until his death in 1941. In her unpublished memoir, she described how they came to Dublin in search of clean mountain air on doctor's orders and discovered they had "plunged into a hospitable but distinguished community." She wrote of her new home's contrasts, "Where else, we asked each other, after a day of roughing in the open, could one dine in full dress among sophisticated surroundings, only the next evening to picnic in the studio of a famous artist?" Indeed, "Where else could one sleep on a mountaintop and lunch the next day with Ruth St. Denis, the dancer, or a collector of Greek vases?"[1]

Monadnock's appeal to painters and writers never waned, but much of the intense literary activity associated with the

Latin Quarter was transferred to the MacDowell Colony in Peterborough, seven miles away.[2] The focus of Dublin's literary endeavors was *Yankee Magazine*, whose circulation grew from 7,000 in 1946 to almost half a million by 1970, making it the village's main employer, most recognized industry, and something of a national fount for the dissemination of New England folklore and nostalgia.

Dublin also flourished musically. Serge Koussevitzky, conductor of the Boston Symphony and founder of Tanglewood, was a frequent visitor to The Briarpatch, Louise Shonk's house on Snow Hill, and to Twain's old haunt at Lone Tree Hill, as was the violinist Jascha Heifetz. In 1927 Koussevitzky conducted a piece by Dubliner Edward Burlingame Hill, a "delicate, colorful, and refined score" based on "the beautiful and gentle poem" by Amy Lowell, "Lilacs." "It was the first new American piece heard in Koussevitzky's initial season."[3] Koussevitzky also premiered Hill's three symphonies and smaller pieces. George Luther Foote's suite *In Praise of Winter* was introduced by the Boston Symphony Orchestra under Koussevitzky in the 1939–40 season. Foote often hosted fellow composer and critic Virgil Thompson at The Thistles. Paul Robeson stayed with artist Alexander James and performed at the James Studio in 1922.

Dublin, which had entertained President Taft and had been the summer home of one of his cabinet members, as well as the holiday refuge for the ambassadors of King and

Brewster gardens

Kaiser, briefly entered the world spotlight with two Dublin Peace Conferences, in 1945 and again in 1965. These were the brainchildren of Dublin resident Grenville Clark.[4] The first gathering brought together fifty prominent Americans – including Norman Cousins, Kingman Brewster, and Supreme Court Justice Owen Roberts – to suggest revisions to the United Nations Charter and to seek means to control the proliferation of atomic weapons.[5] The second peace conference was held at the studio of Alexander James.[6]

The Joseph Lindon Smiths continued to entertain notable guests such as Amelia Earhart and the Countess Mountbatten until their deaths, he in 1950 and she in 1965. Another circle of artists and writers centered on Alexander and Frederika James in the Samuel Davison house in the Lower Village.[7]

In the architectural sphere, with the exception of Pompelia, the age of grand summer cottages staffed by servants was over. Yet Dublin's patronage of outstanding domestic design continued in the building of more modest houses.

Not surprisingly, the Georgian and Colonial styles that were introduced at the turn of the century remained popular. In 1924 when the nineteenth-century Asa Morse farmhouse (one of many structures on the extensive Monadnock Farms established by the Leightons) burned down, the New Haven firm of Norton & Townsend built a replacement on the old foundations. The house is a two-story, white frame Colonial, featuring a projecting porch supported by slender paired columns of Federal delicacy. The same architects were probably responsible for a single-story cottage built at the same time for the Frederick Brewster family, who had purchased the Leighton property in 1925 and re-named it Morelands.[8]

Mrs. Margaret Brewster, a nationally known horticulturist and vice president of the Garden Club of America, commissioned Boston landscape architect Arthur Shurcliff to lay out extensive gardens around the house. Shurcliff was soon to be appointed the landscape architect for Colonial Williamsburg and his interest in formal design was reflected in what was to become Dublin's most famous garden, now gone. The following year, Shurcliff was retained by Frederika James to help plan her garden in the Lower Village, and he also did some work for Daniel K. Catlin and Jasper Whiting.[9]

Consciously reflecting two of the most important English gardens of this century, Hidcote and Sissinghurst, the Brewster gardens were laid out in a series of rooms, protected from the harsh climate by hedges of Canadian hemlock, filled with flowers from greenhouses and providing continuous color from spring to frost. Accentuated with statuary, they included a long terrace with an Italian well, a great lawn of twelve acres framing a view of Monadnock and the lake, a rock garden featuring an Etruscan bird bath, and a round garden with a vista to a waterfall garden. Additional garden rooms were devoted to certain styles, including an English sunken garden, a French garden used as an outdoor theatre, and an Anglo-Italian "plaisance," as well as a hidden statuary garden with a statue of St. Francis brought back from Siena. Each garden had its own planting scheme – often emphasizing a particular color – employing an incredible range of annuals and perennials. The plan was by Shurcliff, but Margaret Brewster devoted almost thirty years to the garden's development and perfection, sometimes employing as many as fifteen gardeners.

Just across the Keene Road from the new building at Morelands, a house and barn built in 1883 were updated in the Colonial style. These were originally constructed as farm buildings for Richard T. Parker, although Parker's house was torn down in 1907 when the first Daniel Catlin hired Charles Platt to design a house for his son. And it was the younger Catlin who engaged Boston architect Richard Wigglesworth to add such features as Palladian windows, an octagonal cupola, and more period detailing to both house and barn, which were joined by a classical pergola.[10]

Another studio remodeling during this period is found on Gerry Road – a 1929 conversion of a barn built by sheep farmer Samuel Fisk sometime in the 1790s. The architect was Albert Harkness, a talented Providence designer.

Harkness was the son and grandson of classics professors at Brown University, and, like John Lawrance Mauran, attended M.I.T., and then worked for Delano & Aldrich, as well as for McKim, Mead & White. Harkness made his reputation as a designer of houses that were "a mixture of 'Provençal,' Renaissance (especially English) and American Colonial," but at the time he was working in Dublin, he ventured into Modernism.[11] The studio at Robinwood, as Gerry called his place, happily combines an eighteenth-century agricultural building with the comfort and flair of the Dublin

art colony. The shingled studio has a monumental two-story window of 120 panes where the barn doors once hung, and three small circular windows at second-story level. Like the best of Harkness's domestic work, the Gerry studio stresses informality rather than the pompously ceremonial.

The year 1929 also saw the construction of yet another

Gerry Studio

new structure on the foundations of an earlier house, the nineteenth-century Timothy Twitchell homestead: Ox-Road Cottage, a guesthouse on the estate of Mrs. William Amory. The house was attributed to Lester S. Couch, a draftsman and later partner in the firm of Little & Browne.[12] Couch designed a number of public buildings in Danvers, Massachusetts, including the Masonic Temple and the Peabody Institute; he also did the Masonic Temple and the First Congregational Church in Salem. Arthur Little was involved in the enlargement of Trinity Hall three years earlier. Ox-Road Cottage is a one-and-a-half-story Arts & Crafts house, with brick and shingle walls, multi-paned casement windows, and prominent overhangs.

A more overtly English flavor is evident in the summer residence built by Edward K. Newbegin in 1933–34 at the western end of Dublin on the Old Marlborough Road. In addition to the house's affinities with the Cotswold vernacular suggested by its roughcast roof walls and slate roof, the Newbegin house also had an Italian feeling, emphasized by its formal garden. This Anglo-Italian composition is intriguing when one considers that both the house and landscaping were the work of Joseph Everett Chandler, an authority on Colonial American architecture and the restoration architect for the Paul Revere House in Boston. Thus, in this house in Dublin, Chandler captured an informal formality within a variety of historical sources.

The Newbegin house was designed as a smaller version of the architect's own country house called Manalone in Sudbury, Massachusetts. While few of Chandler's papers and drawings survive, the architect's diaries from 1919–41 are extant and provide us an unusually full account of the building of this Dublin "bungalow." Edward King Newbegin had been raised by two maiden aunts, Anne and Caroline King, and Chandler had built the King house in Brookline in

Newbegin House

1925. The "Dublin mountainside lot" was chosen because of family friendship with Mrs. Kershaw at Stone Pond, a frequent stopping place for the architect and client during planning and construction – the diary lists $2 paid to pull Newbegin's car out of a muddy Old Marlborough Road. It also makes clear that the aunts had more say on the house's design than their nephew. Chandler often bemoaned the aunts' request for more house for less money ("I shall yet go crazy over that $10,000 job. . . . Much easier to build a $50,000 one. . . . Never did such a small house consume so much time!"). The 1933 estimates of $8,000 for the stone house went by the wayside as the aunts demanded an endless list of "refinements" and foolish economies, then opted for expensive plumbing and rubber flooring. In 1936, Chandler offered his formal garden plan to his client as a wedding present. Alas, Edward's hapless fiancée broke her engagement a fortnight before the wedding.[13]

The novelty of the Newbegin cottage seems somewhat tame when compared to the dacha conceived and built by the Russian émigré Gouri Ivanov-Rinov on Pierce Road. This seemingly plain two-story house, with its strong massing, timbered accents, and roofline of varied gables, is the only example of rammed earth (or *pisé de terre*) construction in New Hampshire (his construction guide was a booklet from the U.S. Department of Agriculture that he purchased for twenty-five cents). A son of a former Imperial Russian officer who was the Governor of Turkestan, Ivanov-Rinov built his house between 1938 and 1957 on land given him by neighboring artist Alexander James, with whom he had studied at the Museum School in Boston. Using a stone foundation and a protective covering of stucco, Ivanov-Rinov spent twenty years constructing his solid house with its eighteen-inch-thick walls, confounding the natives while doing so. A theatrical designer and painter of religious icons for Orthodox churches, he operated a summer art school here from 1945 to 1965, the year before his death.

Gouri Ivanov-Rinov and Alexander James

The construction of large summer cottages may have ceased, but the flurry of studio construction demonstrated that Dublin's appeal as a congenial environment for artists had not diminished. Ivanon-Rinov's rammed-earth house and studio was only one part of the artists' community that developed in the Lower Village-Pierce Road area in the 1920s and '30s.

The focal point of this mini-colony was the Federal-period brick house bought in 1920 by Alexander James and

ABOVE: *Ivanov-Rinov House*
OPPOSITE: *James Studio*

his wife Frederika, who restored and imaginatively extended the grounds by means of walled gardens and handsome outbuildings. Like the Lindon Smiths, the Jameses were known for their hospitality, and the house, which they called Innisfree and sometimes whimsically Home James, became a second home for all sorts of artists and literary figures, including Rockwell Kent and Paul Robeson.[14]

James and fellow painter Richard Meryman moved a small building that they used as a studio and classroom from its original location behind the Heald Tavern. James, however, had long wanted a larger studio – not just a converted shed, so in 1945 he commissioned his friend New York architect Eric Gugler to design a new studio a few feet from the transplanted one. The new James studio was constructed with lumber from two dismantled barns, but it achieves an elegant effect by means of simple, vertically-boarded walls and two superbly proportioned full-height windows on the north and east sides. It contains a forty-foot-square, twenty-foot-high studio space, as well as a library, kitchen, and living quarters.[15]

As a traditionalist practicing in the Modern period, the multi-talented Gugler is little remembered today. Despite being fashionably out of fashion, he was a successful architect. In addition to designing similar studios for the sculptor Paul Manship in Gloucester and another in Keene for his friend, muralist Barry Faulkner, Gugler reconstructed the West Wing of the White House, which had been destroyed by fire in 1929. Gugler worked with his friend and amateur

architect Franklin Roosevelt in designing a new Oval Office. Roosevelt even entrusted Gugler with the design of the White House piano. Fittingly, Gugler created the simple Vermont marble tribute to F.D.R. near the Potomac. Like his friend Charles Platt, he was associated with the American Academy in Rome, as a Fellow and later a Trustee; he, Faulkner, and Manship collaborated on a war memorial there. He also designed a memorial to Eleanor Roosevelt at the United Nations.[16]

Hidden in the woods above Lake Road near the site of the painter's studio, is a memorial to Abbott Thayer that Gugler and Manship created in 1941. The studio from which the painter glimpsed his beloved mountain is long gone. In 1936, Town Meeting voted to permanently set aside Thayer's property, which the town had acquired through unpaid taxes, as a tribute to Dublin's most famous artist. The Dublin Garden Club maintained the site for years, but eventually the land reverted to private hands.

The stone memorial, now mostly forgotten and hidden in the woods, remains a powerful talisman, not unlike the cenotaphs raised to great men during the Enlightenment. The roughly round granite boulder is about three feet high and has a slightly recessed, rectangular panel that carries the artist's name and a bronze bas-relief of an eagle. Manship's noble bird of prey has a realistic head, but the rest of the body has been abstracted in an anatomically impossible but visually effective three-quarter view.

At the Jameses, Gugler approached the design as an

entire landscape composition and his application of neo-classical forms to rural New England is also apparent in the garden surrounding the studio. Starting with a columned loggia on the south side, he continued this motif through a series of pergolas that ran around three sides of the garden

Thayer Memorial

and visually connected it to the Shurcliffe landscape of the main house. Gugler also added massive wooden columns to the nearby older studio as part of his overall concept.[17]

Another studio from this period provides one of Dublin's twentieth-century landmarks. The Stone House was modeled on a thirteenth-century monastery where the artist-builder had spent part of her childhood. It stands with Trinity Hall, Pompelia, and Platt's Catlin house as a memento of Dublin's love affair with Italy.

Mary Brush Pierce designed and built the studio for herself in 1948–51, with the help of her brother-in-law, Thomas Handasyd Cabot, Jr. Using only fieldstone and concrete block, plus a few hand-hewn boards from a 1786 barn (along with bricks from a house on Venable Road and some doors Cabot obtained from the Myron Taylor house in Bayville, Long Island), she was able to create a satisfying composition that is both contemporary and romantic. But, unlike the great houses of half a century earlier, this is modest in scale and served as both home and studio for its designer. Here, a substantial presence was accomplished by simple means: a massive chimney in the end wall, the studio window with a rounded arch that breaks the cornice, and the arches forming an arcade where there might otherwise be a plain porch.

The Stone House is close by both Ivanov-Rinov's and the James studios, and collectively they form a remarkable architectural and historical ensemble. Mary Brush Pierce, the daughter of Dublin painting great George de Forest Brush and an artist in her own right, was an ardent conservationist and a leader in the natural foods movement. Her rough stone studio represents the continuation of Dublin's artistic tradition that began with Thayer's first studio in 1888.[18]

Building activity between the world wars may have been modest, but the various studios alone argue that Dublin was still a vital art colony.

Stone House

IT MAY BE too soon to assess the historical importance of the architecture built in Dublin since the Second World War, but it was certainly characterized by continuing the tradition of commissioning first-rate designers. It was this unusual insistence on quality that set Dublin apart from many other small towns in New England.

Most postwar building in Dublin has been domestic, and those houses are scaled much less grandly than those that typified the earlier summer colony. People still summer in Dublin, but the majority of new homes are constructed for year-round habitation (the town's population was 1476 in 2000). Many of these houses are not dissimilar to others built throughout New England, although noteworthy homes have been constructed throughout the period.

Nevertheless, certain vernacular styles persist in Dublin. In 1941, when Paul and Nancy Lehmann designed the School House at the Dublin School, they modeled it on the one-and-a-half-story Cape so prevalent in Dublin in the early years. Although the School House might seem a stylistic throwback, it is not dissimilar to many of the speculative builders' houses found throughout the village and town. A walk down Main Street or a drive along any road in Dublin will turn up a number of what the real estate advertisements call New England Colonial Capes (or other named variants thereof).[1]

New England's perpetual aura of romance has boosted the Cape style nationally, but it is ironic that many houses were, in fact, built from plans that are available anywhere in the country. The former Post Office, erected in the center of the village in 1968, is an example of these popular manifestations of the Cape. Of a slightly higher standard is the "garrison colonial" house on Snow Hill, constructed about 1964 from a plan published by *Better Homes and Gardens* magazine and featuring a second-story overhang – a memory of seventeenth-century Connecticut and Massachusetts houses. Other examples of stock plans include the 1958 Burnett-Ackermann house on the former site of the Leffingwell Hotel, a National Homes product, and the 1966 home of former town clerk Anita Crowell, built from a design supplied by Swift Homes. Assembled Homes of Winchester, Massachusetts offers yet another example of a pre-fabricated house – that on Snow Hill built in 1970–71.

These evocations of the past are found in almost every American suburb and represent a response to the need for affordable housing in styles that are familiar, reassuring, and ostensibly patriotic. While of less interest than the architect-designed houses of the summer colony, these dwellings provide visual evidence of the post-war American dream that should not be lightly dismissed. Such houses, whether from Sears (which began selling houses shortly after the turn of the twentieth century) or other pre-packaged plans, are part of a long-standing American tradition of the do-it-yourself home. One recalls the Souther house that was shipped to Dublin by rail, as well as the pattern books of Asher Benjamin that influenced the plans and details of Dublin houses earlier in the nineteenth century.

The popularity of the log cabin is another example of

114

the American penchant for owner-built homes, as well as a symbol of both pioneers and the Back-to-the-Earth movement. Magazines like *Yankee*, *Down East*, and the now defunct *Country Journal* carried advertisements for manufacturers of log homes – neither indigenous nor popular in the past – and Dublin can boast a few. In the 1970s both Vermont Log Buildings and the Ward Log Cabin Company of Houlton, Maine erected log houses here. Monadnock Log Homes, with the motto "A Notch Above," erected a log house on Old County Road as recently as 2009.[2]

The Cerroni house on Windmill Hill Road built in 1998–99, does have similarities to another type of house that appeared in the New England in the late 1960s: the post-and-beam, which harkened back to the hand-hewn, traditional construction methods of the seventeenth and eighteenth centuries. Some of the better-known examples of these are Timberpeg, headquartered in West Lebanon, New Hampshire, the Shelter Institute in Woolwich, Maine, which markets Hennin Post and Beam timber frame kits, and Grantham, New Hampshire's Yankee Barn. Companies like these usually offer standard designs, but a lot of architects and builders are drawn to the eighteenth-century type of pegged framing. The frame obviates the need for interior load-bearing walls, so they often feature open barn-like interiors. This is true of the Cerroni house, which has a large central family room with numerous windows facing the mountain.

For this handsome Dublin house, David Stephenson of Peterborough drew up a rough plan for the Cerronis and then Doug Bramble of Bald Mountain Design in Walpole, New Hampshire, drew up the design. Stephenson and his crew cut the yellow pine for the timbers, as well as the oak bracing nearby during the summer of 1998; the frame was erected in a single day. As if traditional mortise-and-tenon joinery did not already have medieval roots, old-fashioned tools were used to finish the wood. A story-and-a-half, the house has a

Cerroni House

gabled roof and central chimney, as well as vertical flush siding and a standing-seam metal roof. The effect is that of utilitarian agricultural buildings – simple, strong, and functional. The central smokestack and a shed dormer suggest a family resemblance to a maple sugar house. Setting a barn-like garage perpendicular to the house created a somewhat sheltered entrance area. The gap between the two units quietly frames a preview of Monadnock, saving the really dramatic prospect of the mountain for the living room inside.

The development of the Early American house type represents a desire to recapture the spirit of a supposedly simpler, nostalgically remembered time (never mind that most people are not that interested in investing in modern architecture, nor are banks willing to risk financing avant-garde designs). While housing us in the styles of our ancestors, some of the mail-away homes have become considerably sophisticated. Some companies specialize in recreating seventeenth- and eighteenth-century cottages and saltboxes, while some even feature early building methods: hand-pegged timber framing and hand-split timber shake roofs (like the Bow House, of Bolton, Massachusetts – there is one on the road up to Pompelia, built by Raphael Pumpelly's great-granddaughter). The latter are more expensive than the tract-house Colonials of the immediate post-war period, but examples of both kind are found in Dublin's recent "suburbs" on Boulder and Greenwood Drives off Brush Brook Road, as well as in the Chestnut Hill development off Windmill Hill Road. For the most part, present-day Dublin has been spared the bloated McMansions that have become the scourge of so many New England watering places.

Since the building of the Town Hall in 1882, Dubliners have characteristically relied upon outside, particularly Boston, talent to design their houses. The result is that Dublin contains a range of Modern architectural styles from the 1950s onwards.

One might actually date the introduction of Modernism into Dublin from the house that Eleanor Raymond built for Lillian Chapin on Old Troy Road in 1934. Raymond, a graduate of the Cambridge School of Architecture and Landscape Architecture for Women, was interested in both the past (she was the author of *Early Domestic Architecture of Pennsylvania* in 1931) and in innovative European-inspired design; she also designed the country's first solar-powered house in 1948.[3]

Another woman architect, Barbara Webb, a student at the Cambridge School, built a clapboard cottage on Learned Road near the second Mark Twain home. Constructed in 1951, with the assistance of Handy Cabot, the flat-roofed house was inspired by the work of Harvard architecture chair Walter Gropius, with whom Webb had studied.

Gropius had been the director of the Bauhaus, a school that revolutionized European architecture. When the school was closed by the Nazis, Gropius – along with his successor Mies van der Rohe and a number of teachers and students – fled, bringing the International Style to America. In the late 1930s, Gropius built a home for himself in Lincoln, Massachusetts, which became one of the iconic Modern houses in

116

America. Although he claimed that it was his reinterpretation of the frame New England house, its flat roof, exposed exterior metal staircase, and its slatted sunscreen are far more European than local. It should not be wholly surprising that Gropius's theories – the past should be ignored and that man's environment could be bettered through a reliance on the machine – would appear in a town as architecturally au courant and sophisticated as Dublin.

The Dublin designer whose work was seemingly most thoroughly representative of the International Style was Alexander R. James, Jr., son of the painter. Sandy James's Baker house of 1954, his own house two years later, and the Anable-Hutchinson house of the following year, feature nearly flat roofs, horizontal strips of windows, and a total absence of reference to any past earlier than about 1920. James, however, had studied only briefly with Gropius at Harvard before transferring to Yale, where he obtained his Bachelor of Architecture degree in 1948.[4] Nevertheless, he was influenced at second hand by Gropius through a San Francisco architect named Henry Hill who had completed his degree at Harvard with the Bauhaus master and with whom James worked for a couple of years in the late 1940s. At that time, too, Hill worked briefly with Erich Mendelsohn, one of the other notable European Modernists and another German refugee.

A look at some of the hundreds of houses that Hill

Perkins House

designed in the San Francisco Bay area, but especially those from the immediate post-war period, show how much James's Dublin work was shaped by their association. These homes, from Berkeley to Carmel, have been described as "standard International Style-meets-California Redwood" – rectangular boxes with walls of glass and wide overhanging often flat roofs, "usually on a hill with views, with a wall of windows, a broad overhang or an open rectangular lattice over the windows."[5] So the young James brought a sophisticated European modernism transformed through the prism of San Francisco, back to his home town.

The Sandy James house that comes closest to his mentor's work – and the purest example of the International Style in Dublin – is the house he built for Ralph and Nancy Perkins on former MacVeagh land along Upper Jaffrey Road.

It would be hard to imagine a more dramatic site, as the house has a sweeping view of Monadnock's eastern flank, as well as an unobstructed view east to the Peterborough hills and south to Mount Wachusett. To take advantage of the setting, James devised a long, narrow L-shaped house sheathed in stained vertical redwood siding and with south and east walls totally of glass.

Only one story high, the Perkins house has a flat roof, and were it not for the mitigating presence of the stained wood siding, it might seem as cool and as abstract as anything by that other progenitor of the International Style, Mies van der Rohe. The Perkins house, which James enlarged in the early 1970s is as much a design of national caliber as some of the great cottages built in Dublin. It is as good as the domestic work of Gropius and calls to mind similar houses of the period by Gropius's partner Marcel Breuer and Mies's disciple, Philip Johnson.[6]

The elegance of the Perkins house as an example of the International Style is somewhat compromised by the impracticality of employing a flat roof and great expanses of glass in a climate as harsh as upland New Hampshire's. The limitations of the style became apparent to James before it did to most of his Harvard-trained colleagues, and he soon turned away from the German worker housing aesthetic in favor of a warmer, more personal expression. The redwood walls of Crow Hill, the house he designed for Harvard College dean Francis Skiddy Von Stade were not stained, but left natural and allowed to age. This 1966 composition at the west end of the lake has steeply pitched roofs and looks a bit like a contemporary rendition of an English country farmhouse. Sandy James's transformation into a practitioner of the vernacular seems complete with his 1967 addition to Georgiana Parsons's 1903 studio and his 1973 design for a simple frame house for his artist brother Michael on Pierce Road (the style of which the sculptor called "A.R. James, with sibling overtones"). Having abandoned his Modernist credo, James then shed his practice as well, retiring to write in primitive isolation on the south coast of Ireland.

One of the most important, yet least known, modern houses in Dublin is Oak Hill, situated high above Dublin Lake on an 1800-foot spur of Monadnock. Oak Hill was

118 lovingly, even obsessively constructed between 1958 and 1962 by Professor Ray Winfield Smith, a native of Marlborough, an Egyptologist (although not related to Joseph Lindon Smith), and an authority on ancient glass. Designed by Washington architect James Hilleary, it was constructed of Georgia cypress, featured flat roofs with a tower and viewing platform, as well as a swimming pool blasted from the granite slope.[7]

Smith originally approached a "local architect" about building his Dublin house (presumably Sandy James). Hilleary recalls that his client wanted a museum-quality building, with the best materials (he wanted the house to be maintenance-free), and an endless array of electronic gadgets that would melt snow, ignite fires in the fireplace at a signal from the bottom of the driveway, and heat the outdoor swimming pool. Smith specified thirty five-by-eight-foot embellished bronze panels over the windows to be designed by noted sculptor Harry Bertoia. Smith refused to pay Bertoia's fee and so Hilleary created them. Smith was courted by a number of architectural journals wanting to feature Oak Hill, and he agreed to a story in *House Beautiful* (the piece was to be called "A Home for All Seasons"). The magazine photographed the exterior, but Smith balked at having his furniture rearranged for interior shots. So the house was never published. It was, however, recognized by a First Award from the American Institute of Architects in 1963.[8]

The year Oak Hill was finished, another unusual house called Idlehour appeared in Dublin, built near the site of a Parsons family summer cottage. Designed by Branford, Connecticut architect Richard McCurdy for Sally Stewart Preston and Kendall Preston, Jr., the single-story house, carefully crafted of fieldstone, redwood, and copper, has a crescent-shaped plan that snakes along the landscape like a caterpillar.

Oak Hill

Caterpillar House

The house is 140 feet long, although the plan is semi-circular, spreading out from the fifty-five-foot wide living/dining/kitchen core. This grand two-story space culminates in a prow that looks out toward the mountain. The plan of the central part is a non-equilateral pentagon, the shape of which is echoed in the double fireplace formed of huge boulders. This massive mountain of stone anchors the house much the same way Frank Lloyd Wright's oversized chimneys stabilize free-flowing open spaces that peeled away from the shelter of the hearth. In fact, the polygonal plan – to say nothing of the dominant fireplace and the exposed woodwork – is strongly reminiscent of Wright's late work. And like Wright, McCurdy has wedded his house to the landscape it occupies.

The combination of the warm materials and the undulating, wavy roof contributes to a composition that has a very Japanese feel – as if the mountain that it faces were a calligraphic silhouette on a scroll. McCurdy, a Philadelphian, trained at Yale, both as an undergraduate and graduate, admits he was very much influenced by Japanese design even though he never visited Japan.[9]

But the genesis of the commission was curious, to say

the least. McCurdy was interviewed on the radio in New York by fashion editor and television writer Emily Kimbrough (the architect's mother-in-law). Mrs. Preston heard his talk on modern architecture and contacted him. But the patron–designer relationship, however, was never a happy one. For example, Mrs. Preston started out by buying a number of rugs, sending McCurdy their dimensions, and asking him to create the house around them. Furthermore, she was a woman of ample figure and instructed McCurdy to design a kitchen large enough for her to dance around in it. The Prestons traveled to Wales to buy tremendously expensive floor tiles for the house, and as a result decided they only had money enough to cover the roof with asphalt. After two summers of construction, McCurdy withdrew from the project. Nevertheless, he has always been proud of the house, especially the way in which he was able to nestle it into the landscape.[10]

Somewhat more traditional are two handsome houses designed by Willis Mills, Jr. of the New Canaan, Connecticut firm of Sherwood, Mills & Smith. The first was built in 1969 for Daniel and Moira Burnham at Grand Monadnock Farm near Fasnacloich, the second for the Rev. Samuel and Jessie Hale at Loon Point in 1975.

Daniel Burnham, has been a farmer, politician, and one-time publisher of *The New Hampshire Times*, while his wife was a MacVeagh whose grandparents built Fasnacloich, where she summered. The Burnhams' house is an early example of the "shed roof vernacular" championed by Yale architecture dean Charles Moore and others in their attempt to find a more sympathetic alternative to the International Style. Its architect, Willis N. Mills, Jr., however, had studied at Princeton, and his own 1956 house in New Canaan, Connecticut, caught the Burnhams' attention.[11] Its steeply pitched roof and diagonal siding suggests a New England barn built in a sensitive contemporary manner. At the point where the two main roof slopes would normally meet there is an opening that provides a space for a skylight and indicates the entrance.[12]

The single-story frame house that Mills designed for

Burnham House

Jessie Hale, the granddaughter of Joseph Lindon and Corinna Smith, is part of the Loon Point complex. While the house does not make any stylistic references to Dublin's summer colony past, its gabled roofs, horizontal clapboards, and separate but attached sections suggest an additive New England farmhouse.

Just as so many of Dublin's nineteenth-century Boston architects had attended M.I.T., many of the contemporary architects who have worked in Dublin are connected with Harvard and Yale. One New Haven-trained designer is Allen Moore, who created one of Dublin's most avant-garde designs for his friend Thomas Wright on West Lake Road in 1967. Wright, then of Keene, met the architect on the Caribbean island of St. Croix and asked Moore to build him a summer house in Dublin; he liked the house so much that ten years later he asked Moore to both winterize and enlarge the house for permanent residency.[13]

Just as we saw the waning influence of European Modernism in the work of Sandy James, the same can be said of American architecture in the late 1960s and the 1970s. Not only was the later, more sculptural Brutalist manner of the great Swiss-French master Le Corbusier supplanting the factory-inspired forms of Gropius and his followers, but architects led by Yale's Charles Moore and Philadelphia's Robert Venturi were exploiting vernacular sources and arguing for the incorporation of historical sources. The Wright house could certainly be seen as part of Moore's shed roof vernacular.

Wright House

Compared to the extreme horizontality of Sandy James's Perkins house, Allen Moore's composition includes a variety of vertical shapes and a picturesque outline composed of stair towers, bedrooms, and skylight, all set under 45-degree roof angles recalling, perhaps unintentionally Dublin's turreted Victorian cottages. The house is stained light gray and is a combination of rural informality and the hard-edged design of the time. Although the wood cladding sets the dominant tone of the house, there is a strong reference to late Le Corbusier in the semicircular concrete garden wall. When the concrete was poured, the impressions made by the form boards were left rough, a practice made famous in Europe by Le Corbusier and in this country by Yale architecture dean Paul Rudolph.

The references to barns and other sensible non-elitist buildings became popular throughout the Northeast, especially for weekend cottages. The practicality of traditional frames, wood siding, and steep roofs lent themselves to a new vernacular – a style that mounted a serious challenge to the Colonial as the standard Dublin house type. Examples of the 1970s New England "outbuilding style" are the post-and-beam Colbert house overlooking Stone Pond (1971–72) and the weekend retreat built a year later by George Fales just below the Thoreau Cottage on Burpee Road. The Fred and Marijke Carter house on Charcoal Road was designed in 1973 by Peter Garland, a Harvard and Rome-educated professor of architecture at Smith College. Garland's lakeside domestic composition is sheathed in vertical hemlock siding, and like many similar houses of the period it owes its rustic modernity partly to the influence of the iconic Sea Ranch development in northern California, designed by Charles Moore in collaboration with Donlyn Lyndon, William Turnbull, and Richard Whitaker.

As visually satisfying as these later houses are, they also exert a certain appeal because they respond to the environment in a way similar to their vernacular ancestors. The stylistic and practical lessons inherent in this new direction in regional domestic design were not lost on some of the pre-fabricated house manufacturers (helped in part by the energy crisis and the oil embargo of the early 1970s).

The first to challenge the ready-made Colonial homes so popular in Dublin in the 1950s was Techbuilt, a Cambridge firm founded by Carl Koch and other Harvard design school associates. Techbuilt's philosophy was to provide architect-designed houses at affordable prices. They offered a variety of configurations and materials (they even had a steel model), but their designs were characterized by rectangular plans under low-pitched gable roofs, and they were always identifiable by the windows that reached up to the eave of the gable end. The 1966 Hewitt house in the Latin Quarter is one of the handsomer Techbuilt examples in Dublin.

The success of Techbuilt resulted in the formation of competing pre-fabricated house companies, mainly around Boston, such as Deck House (the Richard Buck dwelling on Meryman Road of 1979–81, and the Ellen Kennelly house on Charcoal Road are but two examples), and the Acorn House of Acton, Massachusetts. One of the first Acorns in Dublin was the twenty-four-by-twenty-four-foot, single-floor, two-bedroom cottage erected for Peg French in 1976 off Lower Main Street (this is Acorn's "Nutshell 900," referring to the buyer's purchase of only the shell; the interior is then designed to suit the owners' individual needs). Mrs. French's sister, Emily Barton Anable, built a larger Acorn nearby in 1976 that she described as "contemporary – very ugly, but perfect for living inside!" Muriel Ivanov-Rinov, long-time denizen of the rammed earth house, moved to an Acorn on Old Common Road near the cemetery. These may be kit houses, but they fit well into the Dublin landscape and are appropriate examples of sensible New England building.[14]

Small houses, both architect designed and pre-fabricated, have recently dominated the new construction scene in Dublin, but occasional large dwellings have been erected as well. When Donough Prince, a Harvard graduate, former Chicago advertising executive, and Francestown dairy farmer, retired to Dublin he hired another Cambridge-based architect, Harold F. Kellogg, to design a substantial and "state of the art" solar house. Prince's house is built on part of the once-extensive Houghton land on the south side of the Old Marlborough Road and has an unobstructed view of the northwest slope of Monadnock. From the road one sees only the redwood siding and the house's many skylights, while the south side is extensively glazed in order to take in the prospect of the mountain as well as to absorb sunlight. Nearby, the south wall of an old barn remaining from the Houghton estate supports a giant solar collector that supplies over half of the house's energy needs.

Another environmentally adventurous dwelling was that built on Windmill Hill in 1980 by Carolyn Demorest, a modern-architecture maven who had worked at *House Beautiful* magazine. This was an envelope house, because it employed a passive technology wherein there is an envelope of air that surrounds the "inner house" that allows hot air from a sunspace (virtually a greenhouse) on the south front to move by

Envelope House

124

convection currents and heat the home. Because of the envelope, as well as the heliocentric siting which catches the winter sun, coupled with superior insulation, the house is heated with less than two cords of wood per year. Envelope houses first appeared in the Colorado Rockies, but Hank Huber of Hancock designed the Dublin example. A former potter, Huber had built New England's first envelope house two years earlier in New Ipswich.

Not every new house in Dublin is as adventurous as the

Renovated Leighton House

Prince contemporary or as ecologically thoughtful a design as the envelope house. Near the Prince house, Donald T. Spaulding, whose ancestors gave their name to nearby Spaulding Hill, built a recreation of an eighteenth-century Massachusetts center-chimney Colonial from a design supplied by the firm of Royal Barry Wills. More than anyone, the M.I.T.-trained Wills can claim credit for the renaissance of the Cape Cod cottage; he understood the essence of the original cottage form and he gave his clients a sense of hearth and home. Yet, curiously, this saltbox turns its back to Monadnock, and its narrow 12-over-12 windows contrast sharply with the broad expanses of glass employed in the Princes' solar house.

An intriguing solution to building contemporary quarters while acknowledging the past came from a decision by the owners of Morelands to remove the large servants' wing from the Peabody & Stearns house. Loring Catlin, a great-grandnephew of the original owner, Mrs. George Leighton, asked Yale architectural historian – and namer of the Shingle Style – Vincent Scully to recommend an architect knowledgeable and sensitive enough to finish the end wall that would be left after the 1926 wing was demolished. In 1979 the Catlins hired Robert A.M. Stern, then professor of architecture at Columbia University and an eloquent spokesman for and practitioner of Postmodernism. The result is a clearly contemporary yet sympathetic complement to the 1888 design by Peabody & Stearns. Alas, this kind of deference to an inherited monument is the exception rather than the rule, so Dublin is doubly blessed by having both a restored Shingle Style landmark and an attractive example of the Stern's work.[15]

Richard Monahon built a new house to replace a 1910 Shingle Style composition by Kendall, Taylor & Stevens on the Old Harrisville Road that burned to the ground in 1978. Mrs. Thayer, the owner, decided to rebuild, so the Dartmouth- and M.I.T.-trained architect created a Postmodern replacement, which like Stern's addition at Morelands, captures the spirit of the original without slavish copying.[16]

Dublin's summer cottage heritage is also reflected in the shingled addition Rick Monahon added to *Yankee* editor

Thayer House

Judson Hale's house on Valley Road in 1984. The first two floors of the Hale house, designed in 1959 by Peter Garland, were almost totally enveloped by Monahon's tower-like wing, the most prominent feature of which is that characteristic motif of Postmodernism, the Roman bath window, which also recalls that of the Amory house of eighty-five years earlier. The top room of the tower is where Hale writes and paints; "But," he exclaims, "one can go even higher. The deck on the top of the house is a wonderful place to see the stars."[17]

Dublin, too, can take credit for its own talented modern architect, Daniel V. Scully. One of Charles Moore's students from Yale, Scully has practiced in the Monadnock region for more than three decades. He has done a number of houses that tap the spirit of the summer colony, some with debts to Charles Platt and others to the Shingle Style, but always with a refreshing, individualistic streak. Most recently he worked on a scheme to build a new tower on the Town Hall that would pay homage to Arthur Rotch's Victorian spire.

But it is Scully's own house on Charcoal Road that is his richest contribution to Dublin's architectural heritage. Calling upon several local traditions – as well as America's love affair with the automobile, the shingled house has a kitchen shaped liked the hood of a 1940s Pontiac. It faces a smaller Greek temple, wherein is a dragster, the engine of which has been replaced by a woodstove; the route connecting the two buildings is outlined by a gasoline station sign and flanking rows of ornamental gazing balls. The garage is part

126

Jud Hale House

Greek temple and part Quonset hut; license plates fill the entablature's metopes, while 55-gallon drums are part of giant pistons that act as classical columns.[18]

As with any architect practicing over a long career, Scully's work has changed, evolved, and some would say matured, from the restless obsession with the car (although a 2009 addition to his house, with its corrugated metal walls and shock absorber columns definitely keeps his romance with the road alive). And Scully has worked extensively in Dublin, carrying out a large number of renovations, restorations, and smaller additions. But the house designed he for William and Susan Barker on Old Marlborough Road represents a kind of apogee of the Dublin summer house.

The Barkers had lived in a Lake Road house built by Sandy James – one that Scully had renovated and enlarged in 1991, in what was the first of his many Dublin projects. "After twenty-nine years of looking at the lake we turned around and discovered the mountain," Susan Barker recalls.

In 1997 we purchased 25 acres one mile down the road. We created our view by clearing 6 acres. In 2000 to experience the land we built a 12 x 12 studio with a wood stove. This building is called "Millennium Lodge." In 2001 we built a 24 x 30 barn. November 2002 we sited our house and started digging the foundation. We chose Dan to be the architect because of his diverse design styles and eclectic interest. Bill [Barker] was general contractor. Both of us worked on all phases of construction.[19]

In that broad meadow with its sweeping view of the north slope of Monadnock, the clients and architect were able to combine several Dublin threads into the perfect coda for this book. Admirers of Charles Platt, the patrons desired something similar to the long H-plan house that the noted classicist used both in Dublin and in Cornish. The narrow plan allows in lots of light, as well as glimpses of the mountain. Yet the house, called On Shore, actually blocks the view from the driveway; there is, in effect, a denial of the mountain, which is remedied by passing into the house and discovering the concealed view. There are a few columns supporting the deeply overhanging eaves, but the house is not in any way Colonial. It is covered in the flexible, textural, and organic material of Dublin's great summer cottage period, the shingle – a happy and appropriate marriage of modernity and tradition.

ABOVE RIGHT: *Scully House*
RIGHT: *Barker House*

Epilogue

DUBLIN HAS avoided much of the economic pressure that threatens more easily built-upon landscapes because it remains a wooded and mountainous upland town. Thanks to enlightened stewardship, unbridled development has not been an issue – Dublin residents in search of a superstore or fast food have to drive a few hills away to Keene or Rindge, while the occasional vinyl-wrapped suburban house is only an insignificant intrusion at present. Any of the various plans for a highway bypass in the 1970s could have wreaked tremendous havoc, but today such road schemes seem as unlikely as they are unfeasible. For now, Dublin's architectural legacy – the early settlement, the many cottage styles, and the revivals and adventurous new fashions – remains secure and pretty much of a piece.

We can take comfort that so many of Dublin's new houses maintain the high standards of their predecessors, and some of these will become the landmarks of the future. The range of the architect-designed houses, the kit houses, as well as environmentally conscious designs, raise Dublin to a remarkably high architectural level for such a small northern New England town. And all that is built upon a solid and often adventurous two-hundred-year-old tradition.

This book has attempted to introduce the world to the richness of Dublin's built history. It is an introduction, but by no means the last word. As both the National Register research and the continued work of the Dublin Historical Society demonstrate, knowledge is the first step toward appreciation; appreciation leads to conservation. As there is so much more material to be interpreted and disseminated, this volume is but one more addition to the literature on that special place called Dublin, New Hampshire.

Pompelia in ruins

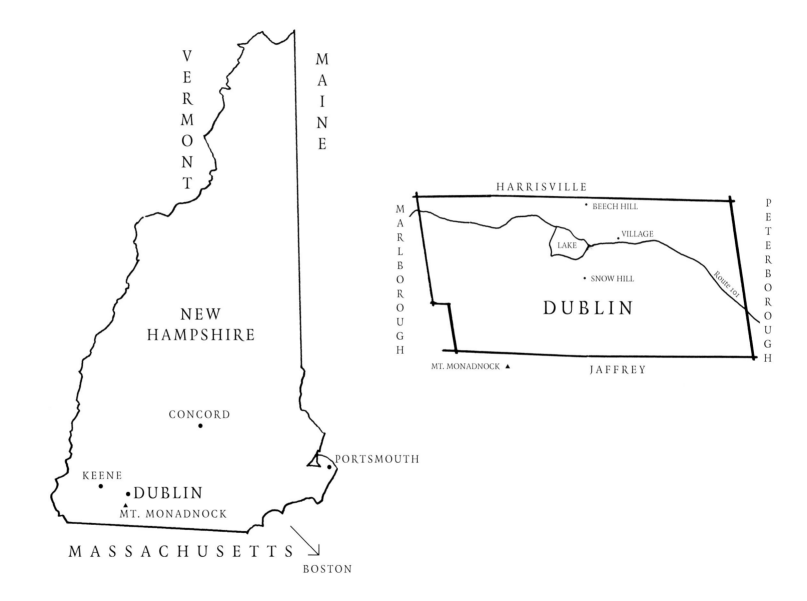

CHAPTER ONE

1   The barns of both houses are gone, one lost to the hurricane of 1938. That both houses were summer homes of educators in recent years speaks of the transformation of Dublin. Bruce McClellan, former headmaster of the Lawrenceville School, added a sympathetic addition to the Thoreau Cottage in the early 1980s, designed by architect Richard Monahon of Peterborough. A chapter, "Thoreau & Emerson," in Craig Brandon, *More than a Mountain* (Keene: 2007) discusses Thoreau's trips to Monadnock.

2   See William Morgan, *The Cape Cod Cottage* (New York: 2006).

3   Cyrus Chamberlain's father, James, was a veteran of the Battle of Bennington.

    The house was purchased as a parsonage for the Dublin Community Church in 1978 and was restored. The west door is a conjectural restoration created by Dublin historian and publisher, William L. Bauhan, son of the Colonial revival architect, Rolf. W. Bauhan.

4   For a general introduction to styles, see William Morgan, *The Abrams Guide to American House Styles* (New York: 2004).

5   Outlet Farm was one of the early summer boarding houses. Much later it was the home of the international lawyer and world peace advocate, Grenville Clark, and was visited by an endless parade of important personages, including Robert Frost and Clement Attlee. The Colonial revival front porch is a turn of the twentieth century addition.

6   Long the home of the painter Alexander James, son of the philosopher William James and nephew of the writer Henry James, the house hosted such cultural and political luminaries as Rockwell Kent, Paul Robeson, Agnes de Mille, and Dean Acheson. From 1972 to 2006, this was the home of William L. Bauhan, a graduate of Princeton and Oxford, who ran a publishing business here. Bauhan also was the co-founder of the resurrected Dublin Historical Society.

7   In 1896 Heald's was reactivated as the Monadnock Hotel, renamed first the Dublin Inn and later French's Tavern, and run as an inn until c. 1940. Not surprisingly, a lot of notables put up at this inn when visiting Dublin, perhaps the most important being Abdu'l Baha', son of the founder of the Baha'i religion, who stayed here for several weeks in 1912. The painter Alexander James and fellow artist Richard Meryman (both students of Abbott Thayer) held summer art classes in the studio behind the house between 1918 and 1922.

8   Levi W. Leonard and Josiah L. Seward, *History of Dublin, New Hampshire* (Dublin: 1920) (hereafter cited as *History*), 24.

9   The Ashby, Templeton, Fitzwilliam, and Acworth churches, along with a similar one at Westmoreland, N.H., are discussed in Robert P. Bellows, "Country Meeting Houses along the Massachusetts–New Hampshire Line," *White Pine Series of Architectural Monographs*, Vol. XI, (1925). Bellows did not mention Dublin (it had long been demolished), but he says these churches "show the wooden country meeting house of a hundred years ago at its best." There is a chapter on the Acworth meetinghouse in William Morgan, *American Country Churches* (New York: 2004).

10 Ernest Hebert's *Live Free or Die* (Hanover, N.H.: paperback edition, 1995) is set in the town of Darby, which is based in part on Dublin. "Upper Darby was a hill town. Hill towns – goddam 'em. They drive the children away from home; they forbade return. A hard climate, poor soil, isolation from the rest of the country had worn down his own kind [Selectman Crabb], river-valley farmers, but it had completely defeated the hill farmers. It had

132

hurt his father when the rich folks took over Upper Darby at the turn of the [twentieth] century, but Crabb figured better the rich than the poor, for a hill town was no place for a man without independent means. These upland towns did not provide; these upland towns thrived with the first generations, which always seemed to be lucky, and then the inevitable bad year would come – not enough rain or too much, or early frost or late frost, or the national economy bad. The valley towns made it through these times, not the hill towns. God might live on a hill, but he didn't favor the common man for a neighbor" (146).

Novelist and Dublin summer resident, Eugenia Brooks Frothignham notes of the fictional upland town where her *Way of the Wind* takes place, "The country had once been a famous sheep raising district, but lack of sufficient water had caused this industry to be abandoned" (Boston: 1917), 65.

11   During the heyday of the summer colony, the Gleason house served as Dublin's second post office, simply called Monadnock, N.H. The house was acquired in 1966 by Isaac Davis White, the only New Hampshire native (he was born in neighboring Peterborough) to achieve the rank of four-star general. A graduate of Norwich University, cavalryman White managed the equestrian team in the 1948 Olympic games in London. During the Second World War, he commanded the Second Armored Division ("Hell on Wheels") under George Patton and led the first American troops across the Elbe River in 1945. After commanding X Corps in the Korean War, White became Commander in Chief of U.S. Forces in the Pacific.

12   The Vermont marble obelisk, on a base of Fitzwilliam granite, in front of the schoolhouse commemorates the twenty-five men Dublin lost in the Civil War. The designer was H. Brennan of Peterborough, who was also responsible for similar monuments in Temple and Sullivan. Erected in 1870, it was moved to the schoolhouse lawn in 1929. Schoolhouses numbered 2, 3, and 4, have all been converted to dwellings.

13   The Piper house is unusual in that it is not connected to its barn just behind it, almost as if such a connection might mitigate the temple form of the block of the house. Nineteenth-century Dubliners were great recyclers, and it is thought that the Piper house used framing timbers from the eighteenth-century William Greenwood house. Piper was a descendant of Greenwood's. Captain Piper was Dublin's school superintendent, a selectman, and a state legislator, while his wife was the artist-illustrator Maria E. Perry. Their son, also Henry, was professor of dentistry at Tufts University. Author and poet George Abbe wrote his novel *The Winter House* while living in the Piper house about 1946.

14   The conservatism of Dublin's early architecture is also apparent in the second church erected by the Trinitarians, an 1877 frame structure that is little more than an enlarged house with a spire added to it – it too a casualty of the 1938 hurricane. The Trinitarian church began a new life in 1978, when the Women's Club deeded the church to the town; it was converted to serve as the Dublin post office.

15   *History*, 93.

CHAPTER TWO

1   The Wilder-Townsend farm would later become the home and studio of George de Forest Brush, one of the leading figures of the Dublin Art Colony.

2   The Piper-Proctor house has been the Dublin General Store since 1984 and is next to the post office (the former Trinitarian church), forming a small center of civic and culinary activity.

3 Mrs. Serena Appleton Morse was the niece of Jesse Appleton, the first president of Bowdoin College, as well as first cousin of Mrs. Franklin Pierce.

4 Monadnock means the "mountain that stands alone" in Abenaki, and is one of the tallest freestanding mountains. The geological term "monadnock" refers to any tall mountain not part of a range.

5 See F. Van Wyck Brooks, *The Flowering of New England* (1937).

6 There is no single comprehensive book on Mount Monadnock. See Allen Chamberlain, *The Annals of Grand Monadnock* (1936), reprinted by the Society for the Protection of New Hampshire Forests (1975). Also, Howard Mansfield, editor, *Where the Mountain Stands Alone: Stories of Place in the Monadnock Region* (Lebanon, N.H.: 2006) (contains a bibliography). Also, Craig Brandon, *More than a Mountain* (Keene, N.H.: 2007), Chapter 7, "Writers & Poets."

7 Harrisville, the mill village and northern half of Dublin, seceded in 1870 in a dispute over the railroad; Dublin's farmers were less enthusiastic than the mill owners about paying for such a line.

8 William Bauhan made the notes from the Leffingwell hotel register.

9 The Leffingwell family also re-opened Heald's Tavern in 1896 under the name Monadnock House.

10 In *The Last Resorts* (1952), social historian Cleveland Amory posits a "theory of resorts": "Generally speaking, the following groups have come to the social resorts in this order: first, artists and writers in search of the good scenery and solitude; second, professors and clergyman and other so-called 'solid people' with long vacations in search of the simple life; third 'nice millionaires' in search of a good place for their children to lead the simple life (as lived by the 'solid people'); fourth, 'naughty millionaires' who wished to associate with the 'nice millionaires' but who built million-dollar cottages and million-dollar clubs, dressed up for dinner and utterly destroyed the simple life; and fifth, trouble" (23). Dublin never developed beyond the third stage.

CHAPTER THREE

1 The Osgoods came to Dublin in 1869. Mrs. Osgood was a pupil of Franz Liszt and produced an anthology of poems called *The City Without Walls* in 1932 (see note 5, *infra*). Her nephew, Robert Pearmain, was the first husband of Nancy Brush, who as Nancy Bowditch, wrote a biography of her father, the Dublin painter George de Forest Brush (1970).

2 Flint Cottage was sold to the Pierpont Flints. Professor Lewis B. Monroe (the founder of Emerson College) and his wife (an Osgood) renovated an eighteenth-century farmhouse, which was torn down in 1936. Another summer tenant of Flint Cottage was Irving Babbitt, the Harvard professor and literary critic; a founder of the New Humanism, he was an important influence on his student, T. S. Eliot, who himself had a Dublin connection – his cousin was Aimée Lamb; Eliot visited his brother at Aimée's house in Dublin in 1946. Miss Lamb was Arthur Rotch's niece.

3 Beech Hill Farm was subsequently owned by former NATO commander General Lauris Norstad who in the early 1970s extensively remodeled the house, eradicating much of its Victorian character.

4 Eliza Pumpelly's husband was the geologist and explorer, Raphael Pumpelly, who moved his family to Dublin from Newport. Putnam was the wife of the New York publisher and the mother of Mrs. Joseph Lindon Smith, who became the doyenne of the Latin Quarter.

5 The Osgoods' daughter Gretchen was married to Fiske Warren,

a disciple of Henry George, as well as national amateur tennis champion in 1893. Gretchen, a beauty noted for her Boston salons, was the subject of a celebrated portrait by John Singer Sargent. Her sister Molly married Robert Erskine Childers, author of the classic pre-World War I spy novel *The Riddle of the Sands*, and with her husband became an ardent Irish nationalist. Childers was executed by the De Valera faction in 1922, but their son, Erskine Childers, became President of Ireland in the early 1970s. Following the death of Dr. Osgood, the cottage was occupied by author Nancy Brush, daughter of George de Forest Brush.

6 The house has been attributed to New York architect Russell Sturgis who summered here in 1884. To add to the name confusion, the likely designer, John Hubbard Sturgis's father was named Russell and his mother was yet another Mary Greene.

7 The Thayer bibliography is extensive, but the standard biography is Nelson C. White, *Abbott H. Thayer: Painter and Naturalist* (Hartford: 1951). Thayer's papers are in the Archives of American Art, and the artist was the subject of an exhibition prepared by the Everson Museum in Syracuse in 1982 that was accompanied by a catalogue written by Ross Anderson. Thayer worked hard to protect Monadnock from encroachments and, working with the Society for the Protection of New Hampshire Forests, he helped secure the first land acquisition of 615 acres on the lower slopes of the mountain. Thayer's early work with animal paintings led to his theory of protective coloration, which in turn was adopted as the basis for military camouflage. See, Craig Brandon, *More than a Mountain*, Chapter 13, "How Monadnock was Saved"; also Chapter 9, "Painters & Photographers."

8 Mary Greene became Thayer's benefactor, taking over his chaotic finances, handling his business, running his art classes, and soliciting students. Victorian reformer and essayist John Jay Chapman stayed in Mary Greene's cottage in 1896 while his wife Minna studied with Thayer, as did Buffalo art patron and museum founder John Albright in 1902. The most famous colleague to occupy Miss Greene's house was George de Forest Brush, who stayed here with his family in 1899, prior to his purchase of a permanent home two years later.

9 For example, Cliffs, a summer house designed by Little for George D. Howe in Manchester-by-the-Sea in 1879. See, Walter Knight Sturges, "Little and the Colonial Revival," *Journal of the Society of Architectural Historians*, Vol. XXXIII (May 1973), 147–163.

10 In 1916 Fairview was the summer home of Mariana Griswold Van Rensselaer, the art historian, social reformer, and biographer of architect Henry Hobson Richardson. The cottage added another link with the artists' colony in 1923 when it was purchased by Richard S. Meryman, a student of Abbott Thayer, Frank Benson, and Edmund Tarbell in the late 1890s, and later director of the Corcoran School of Art in Washington. The Merymans moved to Dublin year round when the Corcoran let go the painting teacher, believing him not modern enough for the school. To make ends meet, the Merymans rented out Fairview in the summers. In the early 1930s, the summer tenant was Claude Moore Fuess, the headmaster of Phillips Andover Academy. Fuess wrote his biography of Calvin Coolidge in the tower room.

11 Raphael Pumpelly, *My Reminiscences* (New York: 1918), 656. In 1884 Pumpelly plotted the trail up Mount Monadnock that bears his name. Higginson wrote a poem about abandoned stone walls on the slope of the mountain called "An American Stonehenge."

12 Higginson's wife Mary Thacher, was also a poet and author.

Barton St. Armand of Brown University, who studied Higginson in connection with a book on Dickinson, wrote, "I have never come across the name of the architect of the Dublin cottage" (letter to author, 2 March 1987).

13 *Peterborough Transcript* (23 June 1881). For the Stick Style, see Vincent Scully, Jr., *The Shingle Style and the Stick Style*, rev. ed. (New Haven: 1971). The first house built along the lake's western shore was Livingston Stone's Lakeview of 1874. In 1896 Taggard sold the house to Ethan Allen Hitchcock, shortly to become the Secretary of the Interior under Presidents McKinley and Roosevelt. Wanting to build a more ambitious house on the site, Hitchcock sold the house to livery stable owner Hiram Carey who moved the house across the frozen lake to its present location at the Dublin School.

14 For a discussion of the Stick Style and its European sources, see Sarah Bradford Landau, "Richard Morris Hunt, the Continental Picturesque, and the 'Stick Style'," *Journal of the Society of Architectural Historians*, Vol. XLII (Oct. 1983), 272-289.

15 Edgewood became the Willcox Inn in 1901. Edgewood appears similar to Theodore Roosevelt's Sagamore Hill by Lamb & Rich of 1884–85. Few pure examples of Queen Anne survive in Dublin, although there are a number of houses that exhibit different wall surfaces and the telltale corner turret, such as the Wait-Mason house on Main Street and Far Horizons, built high on the eastern slope of Monadnock by State Senator Dwight Learned.

16 Rotch is best remembered for endowing the traveling scholarship that bears his name, which still supports study abroad for Boston-area architectural students. Born wealthy, Rotch also underwrote the founding of the Department of Architecture at Harvard. See Harry Katz, *A Continental Eye: The Art and Architecture of Arthur Rotch*, exhibition catalogue, Boston Athenæum (1986).

17 The Town Hall has served Dublin in a variety of capacities: town library, high school, concert hall, and the birthplace of Emmanuel Church. Its Colonial makeover is discussed in the chapter on J. L. Mauran.

The Cambridge-based postmodern architect, Graham Gund, used the original town hall as a template for the signature entrance front of a shopping village in South Hadley, Massachusetts in 1988 (see "The Village Commons, South Hadley, Massachusetts," *Architectural Record* [September 1989] 102). The developer and owner of the Odyssey Bookshop, Romeo Grenier, wanted to create a small town center as an antidote to strip malls.

18 Mrs. Copley Greene built another house in 1890 (probably Stowell Cottage near Loon Point, now demolished), but her final construction project was the home she built on a promontory above the lake in 1900. Lone Tree Hill (also known as Tiadnock, and more recently as High Winds) was constructed for her son, the author and playwright Henry Copley Greene. Mark Twain rented Lone Tree Hill for the season of 1905, the first of two summers spent in Dublin. (See Summer Idyll.)

CHAPTER FOUR

1 It is tempting to speculate that Pumpelly's house might have been one of the rare undocumented works of Charles McKim. His firm, McKim Mead & White, was the leading proponent of Beaux-Arts classicism at the turn of the twentieth century, but some of their early work was in the Shingle Style, including the Low house in Bristol, Rhode Island, arguably the most "modern" of all Shingle Style houses. In her article, "Charles F. McKim and His Francis Blake House," Ann. H. Schiller writes: "There is a gap in Charles McKim's Papers from 1870 to 1886" (*Journal of the Society of Architectural Historians*, Vol. XLVII [March 1988] 5). Schiller posits that McKim began using shingles on his houses

as early as 1873. McKim designed a house for publisher Henry Holt in New Rochelle, New York at the same time, and Holt was an old friend, former schoolmate, and frequent guest of the Pumpellys (as well as the friend of such Dublin luminaries as Ethan Allen Hitchcock, James Bryce, and Henry James). In fact, Holt wrote much of his 1923 autobiography, *Garrulities of an Octogenarian Editor*, at On the Heights. Holt's son married Pumpelly's granddaughter, Elizabeth Cabot, in Dublin in 1922.

The standard work on the Shingle Style is Vincent J. Scully, Jr., *The Shingle Style and the Stick Style*, rev. ed. (New Haven: 1971). Scully wrote the introduction to a collection of papers presented at Columbia University and published as *The Architecture of the American Summer: The Flowering of the Shingle Style* (New York: 1989).

2 Longfellow, a friend of Arthur Rotch's, was trained at M.I.T. and the École des Beaux-Arts. The Portland, Maine firm later designed buildings for Harvard and the Arnold Arboretum, as well as the Cambridge City Hall, and a number of stations on the Boston elevated railroad. Margaret Henderson Floyd wrote a monograph on Longfellow's firm, *Architecture after Richardson: Regionalism before Modernism – Longfellow, Alden, and Harlow in Boston and Pittsburgh* (Chicago: 1994). Both Longfellow and Frank Ellis Alden had worked for H. H. Richardson.

3 In 1950, the top half of the turret, along with the house's entire third floor, was removed when the house was converted to year-round habitation.

4 The scholar-statesman, Viscount James Bryce, the British Ambassador to the United States and author of *The American Commonwealth* (1888), used the Snow Hill house as his summer embassy in 1910, as did his successor, Sir Cecil Spring-Rice. Subsequent renters included Henry White, American ambassador to France and Italy, and Claude Moore Fuess, headmaster of Phillips Andover Academy and the biographer of both Daniel Webster and Calvin Coolidge. The Mason house was bought around 1923 by Cecil Shallcross, an English-born insurance executive in New York, who discovered Dublin through his friendship with Agnes Troup who owned Highfield. Charles A. Platt, architect of several Dublin cottages, designed Shallcross' New York house.

5 Dr. Farnham died barely a year after completing his hilltop cottage. His Maine-born widow, the former Eliza Carey, lived on to endow a new library building in Farnham's honor at the turn of the century, where his portrait hangs. Frank Frothingham, son of the Farnhams' neighbors, acquired the property about 1920. He modified the exterior, removing the central turret, simplifying the chimneys, painted the weathered shingles and the colorful accents, and transformed the gambrel to a hipped roof. One four-story tower remains.

6 After the dissolution of their practice in 1890, Cummings wrote extensively on architecture (for example, *The History of Architecture in Italy* [1904]) while Sears continued to work until his death in 1902. Sears designed the Pilgrim Monument (curiously, a version of Florence's Palazzo Vecchio) for Provincetown. His most famous commission is Fenway Court (now the Gardner Museum), a Sienese palace for Isabella Stewart Gardner, a regular summer visitor to Dublin.

7 Browne built two other cottages near his own, Owl's Nest and Lochstead (1884). Both were Shingle Style; Lochstead was later demolished.

8 Anita Wheelwright came from a well-to-do merchant family in Newburyport. Although she was born in Valparaiso, Chile (presumably on a ship owned by her father), she lived most of her life on Boston's Beacon Hill.

9 The Lampoon building was built in 1909.

The Wheelwright attribution, originally suggested by the author on stylistic grounds, was confirmed by Kay Jensen in a letter to William Bauhan (23 September 1996): "I came into the possession of an early accounting ledger of Wheelright's . . . a Dublin house for Miss Anita Wheelright is recorded there." Wheelwright did a number of seaside resort cottages, but is also known for the many schools he designed for the City of Boston. The first draft of this book was composed at Pinehurst in the summer of 1982, and the author later wrote about the house in the joint Berkeley/M.I.T. design journal, *Places* (summer 1984). The house originally sat on an open rise overlooking the lake, but in 1897 when Mrs. Emma B. Chapman of St. Louis purchased Pinehurst she moved it a few hundred yards to the south to make way for her palatial cottage called Homewood. The house was moved about sixty feet to a new foundation and then restored by Dublin architect Daniel V. Scully in 2000.

10 From 1898 to 1913, Pinehurst was the summer home of Mrs. Chapman's son-in-law, St. Louis architect John Lawrence Mauran. Mauran was no doubt responsible for the 1899 addition to Weecote.

11 George Luther Foote's mother, Esther Manton Foote, later married the Rev. Basil King – who summered at Lochstead. King was the rector of Christ Church, Cambridge, and author of best-selling inspirational books, such as *The Conquest of Fear*. George Foote studied music in Berlin and with Nadia Boulanger in Paris, and later composed such popular orchestral suites as *In Praise of Winter*. During summers in Dublin, Foote was the organist at Emmanuel Church.

12 Vaughan also designed the Foote family gravestones in Mount Auburn Cemetery in Cambridge. See William Morgan, *The Almighty Wall: The Architecture of Henry Vaughan* (New York: 1983).

C. Robertson Trowbridge, former state senator, jazz musician, and publisher of *Yankee Magazine* owned The Thistles from 1967 to 1999.

13 Leighton was president of a bank in St. Louis and chief counsel to the Missouri Pacific Railroad. He had rented W.K. Browne's Fairview the year before, but he was not the kind to move into an old farmhouse. In 1887, he bought John Gleason's popular summer boarding house (the 1831 Brick House) at the northwest corner of the lake and the farm property that went with it. Leighton converted this into a gardener's cottage, and sited his new place nearby.

14 Leighton may have been attracted to Dublin by the Rev. J. C. V. Learned, a Dubliner who became a prominent Unitarian clergyman in St. Louis, but it is likely that it was through his father-in-law, a St. Louis coal magnate with the memorable name of Hudson Bridge, who summered in his hometown of Walpole on the Connecticut River northwest of Keene. Apparently, Mrs. Leighton was consumptive, and so Dublin was chosen over Walpole for its mountain air. The Leightons were joined in Dublin by their relations and friends, the Catlins, the Chapmans, and the Maurans – all of whom would make an architectural mark on the community, and later the McKittricks, Markhams, and Mary Lionberger. Leighton's son, George B. Leighton, was the model for the protagonist in Winston Churchill's 1908 novel *Mr. Crewe's Career* (William Pitt, "The Truth About Mr. Crewe's Career," *Yankee* [November 1938], 10–12, 40–41). Leighton ran for the Senate in 1906, spending an astounding $40,000 – to receive only 28 votes in the New Hampshire Legislature. Leighton was profiled in "Prominent New Hampshire Men: George B. Leighton," *Granite State Magazine*, Vol. II (December 1906), 391–398.

15 Wheaton S. Holden, "Robert Swain Peabody of Peabody &

Stearns: The Early Years, 1870–1886" (doctoral dissertation, Boston University, 1969). Holden also wrote "The Peabody Touch: Peabody & Stearns of Boston, 1870–1917," *Journal of the Society of Architectural Historians*, Vol. XXXIII (May 1973), 114–131; this article includes a checklist of selected buildings by Peabody & Stearns, but does not include the Leighton or Catlin houses. In 1926, New Haven architects Norton & Townsend made some interior alterations and added a large servants' wing, which was partially removed by Robert A.M. Stern in 1979. Monadnock Farms covered 1,700 acres at one point, and included imported Devonshire cows (in the hopes they would produce Devonshire clotted cream). Annie Robinson has written a much-needed book, *Peabody & Stearns: Country Houses & Seaside Cottages* (New York: 2010), in which she thoroughly discusses both the Leighton and Catlin houses. In her treatment of the Catlin house, she notes that when completed "the house comprised 9,000 square feet of living space, with 17 gables, 15 principal rooms, including 8 bedrooms, 5½ baths." Robinson also reminds us that Daniel Catlin's winter home in St. Louis was also designed by Peabody & Stearns.

16 Peabody's pre-eminent position in American architecture was acknowledged by his election to the presidency of the American Institute of Architects in 1901. Four years later – along with his friend and Chicago Fair colleague Charles McKim – he was an incorporator of the American Academy in Rome, an institution that counted George B. Leighton among its benefactors.

17 Again, the contemporary writer Ernest Hebert captures the spirit of the ever-larger houses of the era in his fictional village of Darby: "Like the Salmon house and the Prell house, the Butterworth house of Upper Darby belonged to that Shingle architecture stage of the early twentieth century, great sprawling places put together with generous amounts of local wood by skilled carpenters who would have been happier as farmers. Designed by Byronic architects for baronial clients in the episode between the Victorian and the Modern eras so that Gothic gewgaws coexisted with Japanese roof lines, these were houses with enormous porches and not enough bathrooms, houses with separate and unequal quarters for relatives, friends, servants, and pets. The Salmons, the Butterworths, and the Prells had built their dwellings to rival one another, each bigger than the last" (*Live Free or Die*, 75).

18 Before turning to architecture, Edward Cabot was a successful sheep farmer in Windsor, Vermont. He designed the Massachusetts Eye and Ear Infirmary, the Second Boston Theatre, the President's House and Rogers Gymnasium at Harvard, and the Johns Hopkins University Hospital in Baltimore. Cabot was one of the founders of the Boston Society of Architects and served as that group's president from 1867 to 1901. He retired from active practice in 1896 to devote himself to painting.

19 Stonehenge was renamed High House by composer Timothy Spellman and his novelist wife Levlyn Everett; they used the house as a studio from 1939 until the late 1940s, when they moved to Italy. In 1953, Frank McKenna, the former estate manager, removed the 1904 rear wing of the house and moved it closer to the road for use as his own residence. In 1967 Stonehenge was bought by Martin Kilson, professor of political science and sociology at Harvard, as a summer residence. Aides to British Ambassador Sir Cecil Spring-Rice occupied Stonehenge during the summer of 1913, while he was ensconced at a larger house nearby. (Although Spring-Rice rented the Misses Mason house during the war years, William Bauhan believed that during the summer of 1913, the British Ambassador was at Ty-ny-maes.)

20 While the identity of the designers of some of the larger Shingle

Style houses remains a mystery, the Church Street house was the work of Frederick Stickney, a Lowell, Massachusetts architect who specialized in school, hotel, and residential design. Stickney also designed the town libraries of Lowell and of Manchester, Vermont, as well as the police headquarters for the Charles River Reservation. Ann Elizabeth Hayden, a native of Keene, was the widow of the Hon. Joel Hayden, founder of Hayden Brassworks in Haydenville, Massachusetts.

Dr. Wood was a lawyer, author, and one-time attorney general for the State of Vermont. Wood's wife, Almira, was the great-granddaughter of Moses Greenwood. Their daughter Marjorie married Harvey C. Hayes, a professor of physics at Swarthmore, the director of the Sound Division of the U.S. Naval Research Laboratory, and the inventor of sonar.

21 Andrews joined Herbert Jacques and A. Neal Rantoul in partnership in 1885 and their handsome, nine-story Boston Building in Denver of 1889 is reminiscent of Richardson's Marshall Field Warehouse in Chicago. Andrews designed the Worcester County Courthouse, the Brookline Town Hall, Brookline High School, and buildings for Colorado College. He restored Charles Bulfinch's Connecticut State Capitol in 1913–17, and, along with R. Clipston Sturgis, was responsible for the white marble additions to the Massachusetts State House, 1914–17. Perhaps Andrews & Jacques's most interesting work was the garden called Blair Eyrie done for DeWitt Clinton at Bar Harbor around the turn of the century.

Charles Sumner Greene, one half of Greene & Greene, the important Arts & Crafts designers in California at the beginning of the twentieth century, studied at M.I.T. and then apprenticed with Andrews, Jacques & Rantoul in 1890; he then moved onto to work for R. Clipston Sturgis. His brother, Henry Mather Greene

apprenticed with Shepley, Rutan & Coolidge. The architecture world of Boston was small and closely – some might say, incestuously – interconnected.

22 Frederic Crowninshield was also a first cousin of General Crowninshield. See David Ferguson, *Cleopatra's Barge: The Crowninshield Story* (Boston: 1976), 196–97.

Englishman John Gale Marklove built the organ at Emmanuel, c.1870 in Utica, New York. The tracker-action instrument was originally installed in the Reformed Church at Richfield Springs, New York, and then around 1905 was moved to the Methodist Church at West Winfield, New York. It was located through the Organ Clearing House in Harrisville, and rebuilt in Barre, Vermont, prior to its installation at Emmanuel.

23 The Boston firm of Van Brunt & Howe built another important Shingle Style house for George B. Chase, just over the line in Marlborough. This was published in the *American Architect and Building News* (19 Dec. 1885) and was later named Merrywood by owners Justine and Francis Kershaw. One frequent summer guest at Merrywood was the architect Herbert Browne, partner of Arthur Little. According to an essay about Justine Kershaw (Alfred C. Oppler and Ellen C. Oppler, "The Duchess of Stone Pond," *Historical New Hampshire*, Vol. 38 [summer/fall, 1983]), Browne "had designed a lovely house on the other shore of the lake" [which would be in Dublin]. "Another guest who usually stayed the whole summer in Merrywood was a retired Boston architect who had also built some of the houses around the lake . . . Uncle Herbert [Browne] . . . He built Michael Martin's house." William B. Eddy, *Stone Pond: A Personal History* (White Plains, N.Y., new rev. ed., 1988), 136. Martin was the headmaster of the Montgomery Country School in Wynnewood, Pennsylvania and one of Mrs. Kershaw's circle.

CHAPTER FIVE

1 The term Latin Quarter was no longer in general use at the turn of the twentieth century. Mrs. Smith avoided the term, believing it sounded too bohemian.

2 Corinna Smith was the daughter of publisher George Haven Putnam, as well as the niece of Raphael Pumpelly, Professor Henry Hill, and Thomas Hill, President of Harvard. The Smiths were founders of the Lake Club and served as president and secretary for years. See Richard Meryman, Jr., *The Dublin Lake Club* (Dublin, N.H.: 2001).

3 The Smiths had their guests carve their names on a wooden settle, instead of a conventional guestbook. Some of these names can still be read, including Mark Twain and Mrs. Jack Gardner, who signed her name Isabella.

4 Gardner was a frequent visitor to Dublin and one of the more flamboyant personalities who contributed to the atmosphere of high culture and puckish fun at Loon Point. "Mrs. Jack" first met Smith in Venice, where she espied him on a ladder making a painting of the face of Verrocchio's statue of Colleoni. Smith soon became one of Mrs. Gardner's trusted advisors and he secured some of the major works for her new museum on Boston's Fenway (in vain, she offered him the directorship). Smith wrote pageants for her amusement, and he designed the uniform for her Italian major-domo. The standard work on Gardner is Louise Hall Tharp, *Mrs. Jack* (Boston: 1965).

5 Platt's work is well documented and, given their absence from the office files (Avery Library, Columbia University), Platt's biographer Keith N. Morgan once believed that the houses were not by Platt. The discovery of a signed drawing of the Coolidge house at Historic New England confirms Platt's authorship of the house, and thus makes a strong case for assigning the Upham house to Platt as well. See Keith N. Morgan, *Charles A. Platt: The Artists as Architect* (New York: 1985). Also, Norman Newton, "The Influence of Charles A. Platt," *Design on the Land* (Cambridge: 1971), 372-384. Dublin summer resident and biographer of H. H. Richardson, Mariana Griswold van Rensselaer discussed Platt's etchings in her *American Etchers* (1886). Thirty-six of Platt's residential designs are the subject of Royal Cortissoz, *Monograph of the Works of Charles Adams Platt* (New York: 1913).

6 The same men who planned the Chicago World's Fair founded the American Academy in Rome (with financial backing from Dubliners George Leighton and Franklin MacVeagh) as a center to train American architects in the classical tradition. Platt was both a trustee and president of the Academy.

7 Platt's first architectural commission was for Annie Lazarus, sister of the poet Emma Lazarus, in Cornish in 1893. Cornish was also the site of Platt's own house and that for the author and politician, Winston Churchill. The Cornish colony has been well documented in exhibition catalogues. (See, for example, Shirley Good Ramsey, ed., *A Circle of Friends: Art Colonies of Cornish and Dublin*, exhibition catalogue, (n.p.: 1985).

8 Spur Hill, first named Spur House, is built in the flank of Beech Hill, not far above the original Greene and Crowninshield cottages. Spur House was purchased about 1920 by artist Josepha Backus. Her grandson, John Sewall, built a smaller replica of the main house nearby.

9 Platt's sister was the subject of a portrait by Cornish colonist, Thomas Wilmer Dewing. Painted in Cornish and mounted in a gilded frame created by architect Stanford White, *Elizabeth Platt Jencks* is illustrated in Marc Simpson, Sally Mills, and Jennifer Saville, *The American Canvas: Paintings from the Collection of The Fine Arts Museums of San Francisco* (New York: 1989).

According to Keith Morgan, Beech Hill cost $150,000, including the lot, construction, and furnishings (Morgan, Platt, 244). Beech Hill was acquired by Josepha Backus at the same time she bought Spur Hill. It was part of the Beech Hill Foundation's alcoholic rehabilitation center from 1949–2001. The foundation added several buildings and the main house suffered over the years. In 2007, the entire property was purchased by a group of Dublin residents. All of the buildings have been demolished except Beech Hill house, which was sold as a private house. The Beech Hill-Dublin Lake Watershed Association donated the remainder of the land – 67.2 acres – as a conservation easement.

10 Cortissoz, *Platt*, v. The house was a gift from his father to the junior Catlin, who was President of the St. Louis Art Museum and a member of the Carnegie Peace Foundation.

11 Barry Faulkner, "Charles Adams Platt: Part II," ms. of a radio address delivered on WKNE (Keene, N.H.: 1960), 4 (collection of Mrs. Jocelyn Bolle). Faulkner was another Thayer student, and himself later a trustee of the American Academy in Rome. Faulkner was a successful mural painter, who secured a commission to paint two large murals in the National Archives Building in Washington based on Platt's recommendation. Faulkner painted a mural in the state house in Concord, N.H. that shows Abbott Thayer teaching about protective coloration to Faulkner, Brush, and Alexander James (another Dublin painter), along with sculptor Daniel Chester French. See, Barry Faulkner, *Sketches from an Artist's Life* (Dublin, N.H.: 1973).

12 The quotation about the house is from a letter from Nancy Brush Pearmain Bowditch to William Bauhan, 29 April 1978. This letter would seem to refute Brush pupil Barry Faulkner's recollection that Pearmain's studio-house was burned in a fire, the result of the curse of "a small East Indian idol of evil countenance" that sat on the mantle. Barry Faulkner, *Sketches from an Artist's Life* (Dublin: 1973), 79–80.

Nancy Bowditch wrote a biography of her father, *George de Forest Brush: Recollections of a Joyous Painter* (Peterborough, N.H.: 1970). One of Brush's well known compositions is a tondo entitled *A Modern Madonna* and is a portrait of Mrs. Brush and one of their daughters, with Mount Monadanock forming an Arcadian backdrop. *Recollections* illustrates *The Blue Madonna* (1928) in which Brush's daughter Mary Brush Pierce sits on an Italian Renaissance throne holding her naked daughter Nancy.

13 Rolfe is believed to be the first American ever to teach at Oxford. Rolfe's brother Alfred, headmaster of the Hill School, inherited the house ten years before its acquisition by Silsbee. Another brother, John Carew Rolfe, taught Latin at the University of Pennsylvania and also taught at the American Academy in Rome.

14 Letter from Louise Amory to Henry Mercer, 1 June 1900 (Mercer Collections, Bucks County Historical Society, Doylestown, Pa.). The Little & Browne account notebooks (Historic New England) list the Amory house as having cost $43,495 in 1910, with the builders listed as Hayward Bros.; there are additional costs of $5,739.35 in 1911, including $631.56 for the Mercer tiles; expenses for firebricks, mantels, cornices, and twenty-three "Higgin Roll Screens" are mentioned in 1932 and 1935. The Little accounts also include an entry of $968.20 for "Furniture made by Ross" for Mrs. Franklin MacVeagh's Dublin's house, Knollwood. Little designed a house at 407 Commonwealth Avenue, Boston, for William Amory in 1901 – presumably for Mrs. Amory or commissioned before her husband's death in 1900. Joseph Everett Chandler, architect of the Newbegin house on Old Marlborough Road, was hired by Mrs. Amory to consult on "interior design and alterations to an unfinished ca. 1932 house designed

by Little & Browne." In his diary for September 26, 1934 (Historic New England), Chandler wrote: " [G]o to a vast estate in the woods near Monadnoc in Dublin to advise, for just one day, what to do with a little unfinished cottage by Little and Brown [sic] built 2 years ago except for the interior finish." He referred to Mrs. Amory as "a spry old lady of over 80 (recently had her appendix out!). She showed me some features of her big pseudo-Italian house." In yet another link to Italy, the MacVeaghs' niece-in-law Fanny MacVeagh wrote *Fountains of Papal Rome* (1915).

15 Goodell also designed a four-car garage and chauffeur's cottage as part of Mrs. Amory's vast estate. Remodeled into a summer residence about 1954 by local builder T. H. Cabot, this shingle-covered building, with its long, steeply pitched roof, and multi-paned windows, appears to be an American rendition of the English Arts & Crafts style.

16 Atherton (1863–1945) served on the U.S. Geological Survey expedition to the Grand Canyon in 1889. He designed the First Unitarian Church in East Boston, and according to his obituary (*Boston Herald*, 25 Nov. 1945), he was the "first to adapt and install mechanical sterilization and filtration in pools." Along with Herbert Hale, he entered the 1897 competition for an enormous armory in Providence, R.I. As illustrated in the 11 Dec. 1897 issue of *American Architect and Building News*, the young architects envisioned a medieval castle, complete with turreted battlements.

17 Aaron Copland, who was in residence at the MacDowell Colony in Peterborough that summer, composed *Appalachian Spring* for Graham. In 1961, T. H. Cabot, Pumpelly's grandson, added a sympathetic addition to the studio. John and Elise Fallow added a second story in 1997.

18 Pumpelly built a third building on the summit of Snow Hill – a frame Georgian cottage not unlike the work of Platt in configuration. It was built for and designed by his daughter Elise Pumpelly Cabot in 1889, shortly after her marriage. Elise Cabot was a renowned beauty and a favorite model of Abbott Thayer, most notably in his 1893–97 painting *Caritas* (Museum of Fine Arts, Boston).

CHAPTER SIX

1 Margaret Pearmain Welch, "One Girl's Boston," unpub. ms. Margaret Cushing Pearmain Welch was the niece of Margaret Osgood. She continued, waxing rhapsodic about fishing for pink trout in the lake, raising butterflies, watching the stars at night, searching for garnets in the roadside sands. "The first week in September came upon us unreasonably soon."

2 Lowell owned the Crowninshield cottage (which she called Boomley Lacey) from 1901 until her death in 1925. Her eccentricities set her apart from both natives and visitors. As she told Robert Frost, "I've given up my summer place in Dublin – couldn't stand the people in it, the little men" (Laurance Thompson, *Robert Frost, Years of Triumph* [1970], 233). Lowell was making reference to Frost's poem "New Hampshire":

> Another Massachusetts poet said,
> "I go no more to summer in New Hampshire.
> I've given up my summer place in Dublin."
> But when I asked to know what ailed New Hampshire,
> She said she couldn't stand the people in it,
> The little men. (It's Massachusetts speaking).
>   Robert Frost, *New Hampshire: A Poem*
>   *with Notes and Grace Notes* (New York: 1923).

3 Henry D. Allison, Dublin storekeeper, postmaster, and himself

later Progressive candidate for governor, arranged Twain's rental from the Greenes. While at Lone Tree Hill, Twain wrote *A Horse's Tale* and *Eve's Diary*. Subsequent owners included the artist daughter of Joseph Lindon Smith and later Jane Thaw, pianist and music patron.

4   George Willis Cooke, "Old Times and New in Dublin, New Hampshire," *New England Magazine*, Vol. XX [Aug. 1899], 757–58. Cooke also wrote a biography of Emerson.

A somewhat more cynical view was taken in an unsigned piece, "Dublin A New Hampshire Town that has become a Famous Literary Centre," *Boston Sunday Post*, 4 September 1904. "15 years ago, the literary and artistic colony of Dublin was one of the places where millions simply did not count and the gilded fool had no place. . . . But times have changed, and the ubiquitous millionaire has come in and bought up the place. . . . The old time simplicity and unconventionality are rapidly vanishing, and the tendency is to live on a more elaborate and pretentious scale . . . the presence of a French chef and a half a score of liveried servants seems a foreign and somewhat discordant note up here in the woods."

"The Lake Club, however, was and is snobby to the max. The members once purchased a nearby private inn, a Lake Club official explained, 'to enable us to refuse to accommodate undesirable people.' . . . When they set up the club, for instance, a few of its 250 members purchased all of the land around Dublin Lake. 'The lake now belonged to the summer community and the townsfolk were simply expected to stay away.'" Alex Beam, "Dublin, N.H.: both sides now," *The Boston Globe*, 12 August 2003.

In her novel, *Way of the Wind* (Boston: 1917), which is clearly set in Dublin, Eugenia Frothingham's hostess tells her Boston guest, "You mustn't think that the whole region is as lonely as the part you came through . . . I have many neighbors down by the lake, and there is tennis, canoeing, and even dinner parties if one wants them" (8). Later, the protagonist's dissolute love interest "spoke of buying a tennis racquet, and playing at the Club which a fashionable summer colony had built by the lake" (76).

5   George Foster Shepley, Charles Hercules Rutan, and Charles Allerton Coolidge all worked with Richardson and they completed his unfinished work following his death in 1886. An extremely successful national firm, Shepley et al. designed, among other projects, the campus for Stanford University, the New Orleans Public Library, several buildings at Harvard, Boston's South Station, and the United States Building at the Paris Exposition of 1900. The firm continues today as Shepley Bulfinch. The house was later named Bencliffe, probably by Mary D. C. Thoron who purchased the house in 1965. J. D. Gray Thoron was the dean of the law school at Cornell, and the son-in-law of Dublin statesman Grenville Clark. It was during the Thoron years – 1970, to be precise – when several Black Panthers were guests in the house. Bencliffe became a year-round house in 1985.

6   Emily MacVeagh's life was chronicled by Amelia Gere Mason, *Memories of a Friend* (Chicago: 1918). Mrs. MacVeagh was a great entertainer, hosting such luminaries at Mrs. Jack Gardner, Henry James, and Ambassador and Mrs. Bryce, whom she knew long before they came to Dublin.

7   Excerpts from Marion Schlesinger Whiting's "Irresistible Memoir" were published in the *Dublin Historical Society Newsletter* No. 75 (February 2009), as "Summer Dublin Ninety Years Ago."

8   The Frothinghams bought their land from General Crowninshield's daughters. Mrs. Frothingham had close connections to Boston's literary establishment. Her brother was the publisher George Harrison Mifflin, partner and later president of Houghton

144

Mifflin. Her spinster daughter, Eugenia Brooks Frothingham, summered in Dublin for nearly half a century and became a successful novelist.

9   In the 1904 article, "Dublin . . . a Famous Literary Centre," the unnamed author quotes his unidentified host's argument that Dublin was not a second Brook Farm (summer visitors "were not living on roots and herbs in the open") by noting, "A good many of the houses were designed by Carrère and Hastings."

In 1908, Frederick Law Olmsted visited Dublin in the company of an F. E. Frothingham (Leffingwell Hotel register). As tempting as it might be to speculate that Olmsted was here to advise on the grounds of the Frothingham's Monadnock Hall, the Frothingham is undoubtedly Francis Edward, the son of James H. Frothingham, the builder of an 1885 house on the Old Common.

An intriguing note in this attribution mystery is that in 1919 the pioneering women's firm of Howe, Manning & Almy was hired to renovate the Frothingham cottage. Lois Howe began the practice in 1895, and in 1922 designed and built a winter home for Miss Frothingham in Cambridge. There is nothing in Howe's papers and job lists at M.I.T. to suggest that she was responsible for the original Monadnock Hall. Sarah Allaback, *The First American Women Architects* (Urbana, Ill.: 2008), has a renovation for 1911 for Theodore L. Frothingham, no place given.

10   Van Rensselaer, author of *Henry Hobson Richardson and His Works* (1888), occupied High Wells for several summers after 1900. She also wrote extensively on painting, gardening, poetry, and history, and parts of her major work, the two-volume *History of the City of New York in the Seventeenth Century* (1909), were written here.

The underlying formality of the house was accentuated by the terraced herbaceous gardens laid out by Caroline Schurmeier of St. Paul, Minnesota, who bought the house in 1925.

Albert B. Wolfe, a Boston attorney and noted preservation advocate, bought the house in 1942. Wolfe was especially active in preservation in Dublin, and was particularly involved in the preparation of the nomination of the town to the National Register. A conservation pioneer, Abe Wolfe originated the idea that became the Monadnock Conservancy.

11   Georgiana Parsons's house was known as Lower Farm, more recently Interbrook, and now Maplecote, the house was purchased about 1930 by Joseph Lindon Smith's daughter, Rebecca Malicheff, herself an artist and dancer. Ernest J. Simmons, a professor of Slavic languages at Columbia and biographer of Tolstoy, Chekhov, and Pushkin, subsequently owned the house.

12   Irving Babbitt summered here in 1911–13, while writing *The Masters of Modern French Criticism*. Artist Josepha Backus later owned the house.

13   Lavalle was the brother-in-law of Massachusetts Governor Curtis Guild, and evidence of his gilt-edged connections include being prepped at St. Paul's School and being buried in Mount Auburn Cemetery. He is also credited with a school in Great Falls, Montana, of 1894. The house that Lavalle designed for Henry P. King at Pride's Crossing was described in *The Boston Daily Globe* (3 May 1889) as having "the appearance of an English house. It is partly of wood and partly stone, and the roof has so many gables that one is almost forced to believe the architect was desirous of equaling in this respect, Salem's famous 'house of seven gables.' With a circular tower fortified with battlements, and lighted through diamond-paned windows, the house presents a most picturesque appearance."

14   Earle G. Shettleworth, Jr., *The Summer Cottages of Islesboro, 1890–1930* (Islesboro, Maine: 1989) 102.

Lavalle designed a carriage house in the same vein, and was

undoubtedly responsible for Foothill Farm, the farmhouse and barn complex which Mrs. Amory, widowed in 1900, added to her estate on the other side of Old Troy Road in 1914.

Mrs. Amory was, of course, the builder of the Italian castle Trinity Hall in 1910–11. In 1910, Mrs. Amory built an even larger house up the hill, while the original home was rented to summer tenants, the first of whom was Senator Albert Beveridge of Indiana (who wrote much of his *Life of John Marshall* in Dublin). Henry Adams rented the house in 1915.

Mrs. Amory, along with her son-in-law the Rev. George Weld, claimed hundreds of acres of land on the slope of Monadnock that they quietly bought from illegal squatters. Her plans to build a road up the mountain and sell house lots galvanized Abbott Thayer into the first attempts to preserve the mountain. In a letter-writing campaign, the painter compared the development scheme to "carving your name on the ceiling of the Sistine Chapel." Rosemary Conroy, "A Man and His Mountain: How an Artist's Effort Led to the Permanent Preservation of Mount Monadnock," *Forest Notes* [winter 2008], 7.

15 Richards, who rented from Henry Hill, was the son of the Newport-based marine painter, William Trost Richards. Theodore Richards' daughter Grace was a painter and a student of Alexander James; she married James Conant, later the president of Harvard.

16 Henderson, author of texts on England and Germany (his wife was the English-born daughter of a German baron, von Bunsen, eponym of the Bunsen burner), served as his own architect. Henderson's Owlwood of 1902 had both Georgian details and shingle siding. A large house, but in typical Dublin fashion it bespoke a more comfortable by-the-lake summer camp than it did of the grander attempts being built in the town at the same time. The barn was long the studio of Henderson's daughter Frances, a Boston sculptress.

17 *New Hampshire Farms for Summer Homes* 1st ed. (n.p.: 1902), 44.

18 Richard Meryman documented the history of the Dublin Lake Club in *The Dublin Lake Club – Centennial History* (Dublin, N.H.: 2001). Meryman, biographer of Andrew Wyeth, Louis Armstrong, Marilyn Monroe, and Joan Rivers, and the son of the Dublin painter, lives at the Browne house (Fairview).

CHAPTER SEVEN

1 *Dublin Days*, 131, 127. The original house was built by a Revolutionary War soldier and blacksmith, but it is not known why the Uptons did not tear down his somewhat plain farmhouse.

2 The Hite Art Institute at the University of Louisville owns a watercolor drawing entitled *Round Temple of the Tiber*, signed "J. L. Mauran, Rome, Apr. '90" (gift of Thomas J. McCormick, professor *emeritus* of Wheaton College).

3 An undated newspaper clipping that appeared in a St. Louis newspaper at the time of the engagement described Isabel Chapman as "a distinct and aristocratic beauty." The writer went on to praise the architect: "Mr Mauran . . . has youth and good looks, he has talents and brains, but best of all he has tact. . . . Everyone who knows him has a pleasant word for him."

4 One might argue the Village Improvement Society was Mauran's cover, and since his work was not costing the town anything, there was little or no opposition to his vision of what the center of Dublin should look like. Village improvement societies, and the impetus behind them, could also be interpreted as elitist – the work of wealthy outsiders or newcomers who knew what was best for the town (this may have been the case especially in areas

where "colonial" towns were being settled by immigrants who were non-Yankees, particularly not Protestants, and perceived as unaware of those values that contributed to the soul of New England). Once again, Keene native and Dartmouth writing professor Ernest Hebert captures the tensions between natives and those from somewhere else who saw themselves as the defenders of New England culture. "Center Darby Village.... In contrast to the old cemetery, the grass on the common was well tended and already beginning to green up; the fine eighteenth- and nineteenth-century houses surrounding the common had never looked better. The reason, in the language of the times, was gentrification. Educated, prosperous people from downcountry had moved into the neighborhood. The new people (which was the local term for anyone whose family has not been in Darby for at least two generations) liked to fix things up, and they had the money to get the job done. Unlike the natives, the new people believed in the idea of New England, even if the idea wasn't exactly true to the place, whereas the natives believed in the place and lacked any true idea of that place" (*Live Free or Die*, 67).

5   Mauran designed and built a Georgian dollhouse for his daughter Isabel (born at Banjo Cottage in 1894) that was 28 by 92 by 48 inches high, complete with a pedimented, tabernacle-frame entrance and Mauran-created furniture.

6   The library was expanded to the south side in 1999 with what some critics have labeled an insensitive and thoughtless addition, designed by Peter Tennant of Manchester.

7   It was in 1900 that Mauran left Shepley, Rutan, the architects of the other McKittrick (Markham) house on Snow Hill. Did the young Mauran work on Knollwood or the earlier Hugh McKittrick house? All the Dublin–Boston connections would suggest so. Mauran worked in both the Chicago and St. Louis offices of the firm at the times the houses were built, and he might have brought the Dublin commissions to the office; a case can be made for his being the designer of the Hugh McKittrick house for fellow St. Louisans, yet the house shows the strong influence of the Boston office, as well as a suave assuredness not shared by Mauran's domestic work in Dublin.

8   One of Snow Hill's tenants in the early years was Mrs. Marshall Field – no doubt another Mauran Chicago connection.

Wyeth is best known as the designer of the first Oval Office in the new West Wing at the White House in 1909, done for Dublin summer visitor William Howard Taft. Wyeth also designed the Pullman House (now the Russian Embassy) and the Francis Scott Key Bridge.

"There is a persistent oral tradition that the German Embassy was at the McKittricks' house in the summer of 1915, when the British Ambassador was at the Misses Masons" (John W. Harris, to author, 18 December 2009). Count Von Sternberg had rented Holy Wells in 1907, and his successor as German Ambassador (1908–17), Johann Heinrich von Bernstorff, may have been in Dublin sometime in the summer of 1916, perhaps at Ty-ny-maes (William Bauhan, undated index card sent to author, W. L. Bauhan papers, Dublin Historical Society; The Town History notes that "[V]on Bernstorff, German Ambassador visited Dublin late in the season of 1916," 675). Von Bernstorff was expelled by Woodrow Wilson the following year, but his appearance in Dublin while Germany was fighting the Allies led to the unsubstantiated legend that the German chose Dublin because its high altitude made it ideal for communicating with U-boats off the New England coast. Von Bernstorff was, however, involved in various plots to disrupt American and Canadian commerce (see *Memoirs of Count Bernstorff*, New York: 1936). In her

Interesting People, Corinna Lindon Smith recalled, "Count von Bernstorff's presence in Dublin, visiting a neighbor produced an uproar. He was informed curtly to keep off the main roads and was socially ignored. . . . It was not until much later that it developed that von Bernstorff's purpose in coming to Dublin was to have a secret meeting with Wilson at the President's request, in some out-of-the-way locality accessible to both Dublin and Cornish" (Norman, Okla.: 1962). In the 1930s the McKittrick house/Snow Hill became the Lockwood Inn.

9 An interior photograph of Homewood appeared in a contemporary issue of the *Architectural Record*. Many of the house's dormers were replaced by skylights in 1975, but the house burned down in 2007 and was replaced by a "custom built contemporary," which one could hope to live in without an army of servants. The estate also had a farmhouse-stable nearby, also by Mauran. Constructed in 1899, this has a square plan and a hipped roof – Mauran's attempt at the vernacular in a utilitarian structure? This was remodeled by Peterborough architect Gordon Sherman in 1970–71.

10 *New Hampshire Farms for Summer Homes* 1st ed., (n.p.: 1902), 44.

11 *New Hampshire Farms for Summer Homes* 6th ed., (n.p.: 1908), 33. Mrs. Mauran bought Hitchcock's imposing mansion in 1916; it was torn down around 1948.

12 Mauran's life in Dublin is best captured in the several photograph albums that he filled between 1898 and 1923. Mauran was an enthusiastic photographer, as well as an early fan of the home movie camera. His snapshots document Dublin, St. Louis, and vacations at Lake Placid, Palm Beach, and in Europe, plus family canoeing, sailing, horseback riding, and motorcars. These include an August 1905 garden party at the Leightons' Morelands, complete with a stage and people costumed as angels and Indians, as well as a September 1906 production of *Alice in Wonderland* at Brush Farm.

13 The great church designer Ralph Adams Cram began his architectural career as a draftsman for Rotch & Tilden in 1881, the year they designed the Dublin Town Hall. Twenty-five years later Cram would build one of his finest small parish churches, All Saints in Peterborough. Our Lady of the Snows was converted into a house in 2004; the architect of the renovation was Daniel Scully.

14 Porter was Dublin's last blacksmith. While early Colonial Revival, the gambrel roof (and dark color scheme) recalls some of the modest Shingle Style cottages, such as the Emmanuel Rectory. John Gunther, a Hancock architect remodeled the Greenwood house and added a one-story wing in 1940. This work was done for Millard "Spook" and Dorothy Worcester, who acquired the house in 1930, the year Mrs. Worcester began almost seven decades of service as the town librarian; Mr. Worcester operated Worcester's Garage in the center of Dublin for forty-three years.

15 Mrs. Aldrich was the daughter-in-law of poet, editor, and novelist Thomas Bailey Aldrich. In 1951, The Kingdom, a religious community, acquired the house; they have made extensive additions.

16 Chester Holmes Aldrich and William Adams Delano were both products of Columbia University and the École des Beaux-Arts. In addition to the Walters Gallery in Baltimore (1910), they designed the Colony Club (1916), the Union League Club (1936), and La Guardia Marine Air Terminal (1940), all in New York, as well as houses for John D. Rockefeller, Vincent Astor, and Otto Kahn. Aldrich was the Director of the American Academy in Rome from 1935 to 1940. The house was commissioned by three women, one of whom was Aldrich's sister.

17 Kilham attended M.I.T. and studied in Europe on a Rotch

Traveling Scholarship. An avid historian, he wrote both *Vice Regal Architecture in Mexico* (1927) and *Boston after Bulfinch* (1946).

18 The Rand house was on the site of an early farmhouse that had been remodeled in 1889 as a summer cottage by Keene physician H. K. Faulkner (uncle of the muralist, Barry Faulkner). The Rand house was later owned by Justine Catlin Eaton, granddaughter of Daniel Catlin, patron of Peabody & Stearns. Her husband, Fredrick, a prominent New York lawyer, was chairman of the U.S. delegation to the 1960 Geneva disarmament talks.

19 Skyfield is just over the line into the town of Harrisville, but like its neighbor Fasnacloich, it was part of the Dublin's summer colony in spirit and intention. Howe's firm was Howe, Manning & Almy. She was among the earliest female graduates of M.I.T. and was the second woman elected to the American Institute of Architects (her sponsor was Robert Swain Peabody) and first woman elected to Fellowship in the Institute (1931). She and her partners did many Georgian houses in Boston and Cambridge (as well as the Robert P. Bass house in Peterborough, 1928). She was co-author with Constance Fuller of *Details of Old New England Houses* (1913). See Gail Morse, "The Firm: A Study of the First Women's Architectural Firm in Boston: Howe, Manning and Almy" (unpub. master's thesis, Boston University, 1976); also, Sarah Allaback, *The First American Women Architects* (Urbana: 2008), 104-117, has an extensive list of commissions, although not the two in Dublin (another instance of Dublin "under the radar," intentionally or by happenstance?). See also Doris Cole and Karen Cord Taylor, *The Lady Architects: Lois Lilley Howe, Eleanor Manning, and Mary Almy, 1893–1937* (New York: 1990); Taylor and Cole identified 426 projects by the three designers.

20 Frothingham's autobiography, *Youth and I* (Boston: 1938) tells of the younger days, but not of Stone Pond. "Here she built in 1932"

(William D. Eddy, *Stone Pond, A Personal History*, 3rd rev. ed. [White Plains, N.Y.: 1988], 57). Allaback lists the house in Cambridge for Eugenia Frothingham (*First American Women Architects*) but mentions neither Howe's purported renovation for her parents at Monandnock Hall in 1919 nor High Meadows.

Frothingham's novels include *Turn of the Road* (1901), *The Evasion* (1906), *Her Roman Lover* (1911), *The Way of the Wind* (1917), and *The Finding of Norah* (1918).

Miss Frothingham never married and is supposed to have remarked, "My tombstone should be inscribed: Here lies Miss E. Frothingham who might have been Mrs. Soandso or Mrs. Thusandsuch or Mrs. Severalothers" (James Putnam, e-mail to author, 23 July 2009).

"After the 1938 hurricane, however, she became more melancholy. She had her driver bring her up to look at the damage. The house was untouched (as were the Kershaw buildings) but the devastation to the woods was so bad she had him drive her back, never to return." (Eddy, *Stone Pond*, 57). Frothingham sold High Meadows to Henry and Hayes Brigham. Mrs. Brigham gave the house to her physician, George Waring of Cambridge. Justine Kershaw was the daughter of publisher Henry Houghton.

21 Parsons, as noted earlier, was Curator of Prints at the Library of Congress. After Parsons's death in 1915, his widow Agnes actively farmed the place until her death in 1934. She buried $4000 worth of gold coins, which were uncovered by her son almost a decade later – only to have the gold confiscated by the federal government. Abdu'l Baha, the son of the founder of Baha'i faith, stayed here during a visit to the United States in 1912.

22 Thea Brush Cabot confirmed the Parsons–Forbes link, interview, 10 Aug. 1984.

23 The summer residence that sociologist Jeffrey Brackett built for

himself in 1915 should be mentioned, although his Swiss chalet is so unusual for Dublin as to defy characterization (other than a certain Stick Style affinity). Director of the School of Social Work at Simmons College in Boston, Brackett employed gargantuan brackets in a rather unorthodox manner – for visual effect rather than structural support, suggesting an intentional pun on his name.

CHAPTER EIGHT

1 Whiting, Marion S., *Irresistible World* (n.d.: [c. 1955]), unpublished memoir in the collection of the Dublin Historical Society.

2 America's oldest artists' colony, MacDowell was founded in 1907 by composer Edward MacDowell and his pianist wife, Marian. It now has thirty-two studios. The most famous MacDowell Colony residents were probably Leonard Bernstein, Aaron Copland, and Thornton Wilder (who forever put Peterborough on the map when he wrote his play *Our Town* while at MacDowell; Grovers Corners is everywhere and any place, not Peterborough, yet the link has been indelibly made in people's minds). Yet the Peterborough–Dublin town line was not a wall. Poet Edwin Arlington Robinson occupied a studio at MacDowell for twenty-three summers, whence he could see Monadnock and about which he wrote a poem. Martha Graham, for whom Copland wrote his *Appalachian Spring* ballet, was staying at the Pumpelly Studio.

3 Hugo Leichtentritt, *Serge Koussevitzky: The Boston Symphony Orchestra and the New American Music* (Cambridge: 1946), 31, 18.

4 Clark was an international lawyer, a drafter of the United Nations Charter, and author of *A Plan for Peace* and *World Peace Through World Law*. He was an advisor to four presidents, founder of the Military Training Camps Association in the First World War, and author of the Selective Service Act of 1940. Clark is depicted on the thirty-nine-cent postage stamp, issued 20 March 1985.

5 Cousins was the editor of *The Saturday Review*, while Brewster later became president of Yale; also in attendance were Alan Cranston and New Hampshire politico Robert P. Bass. The meeting published The Dublin Declaration and led to the founding of the United World Federalists.

6 Clark's home at the old Eli Morse homestead saw a constant parade of important visitors, including Robert Frost, Clement Attlee, James B. Conant, and Felix Frankfurter. Clark's protégé, Alan Cranston, became a senator from California and presidential candidate.

7 James was the son of philosopher William James and the nephew of the writer Henry James.

8 Frederick Brewster's family owned the Brewster Body Works in Springfield, Mass. Rolls Royce, the venerable English automotive marque, assembled cars in the United States from 1920 to 1931. "Those cars were known as Springfield Rolls . . . in 1926, Rolls-Royce bought Brewster, an American coachbuilder with a reputation for the highest-quality bodies." (*Automobile* [September 2009], 102).

9 The Morelands gardens were described in detail in a typescript, "Factual History of Morelands," written by Margaret Brewster in 1953; this was the basis for the write-up of the gardens in James M. Fitch and F. F. Rockwell, *Treasury of American Gardens* (New York: 1965), 80–81. The authors noted that Morelands was "one of the most famous of New England's larger gardens," and they titled their piece "Garden of Many Facets." Shurcliff (1870–1957) studied at M.I.T. and at Harvard with Charles Eliot; he was associated with Olmsted Bros. from 1896 to 1905. "Autobiography of Arthur Asahel Shurcliff 1870–1957," a typescript written in

1943–47 (Historic New England), lists the Brewster, Catlin, James, and Whiting projects in an index, "Names of Clients," but no dates are given.

10 Wigglesworth was a cousin of Dublin artist Richard Meryman. The barn became the studio of artist Thomas Blagdon, Daniel K. Catlin's nephew by marriage.

11 William H. Jordy and Christopher Monkhouse, eds., "Albert Harkness," *Buildings on Paper: Rhode Island Architectural Drawings 1825–1945* (Providence: 1982), 216. Jordy's write-up of Harkness is the most complete description of the designer's career to date. Harkness (1896–1981) designed a number of schools (including Central-Classical High School, 1963), a factory showroom for Gorham Silver Company, and many country houses for wealthy clients in Rhode Island, most of which were inspired by French châteaux, Cotswold manors, Colonial America, and the English Regency. One of his sons, John C. Harkness, was a founding partner, along with Walter Gropius, of The Architects Collaborative.

12 Amory Glenn, letter to William L. Bauhan, 12 Feb. 1987.

13 Timothy Orwig has written a dissertation on Chandler for Boston University ("Material Things Worth While: Joseph Everett Chandler, the Colonial Revival, and the Preservation Movement" [2010]). Orwig transcribed Chandler's diaries, now at Historic New England.

Perhaps it is unfair to overstress the link of Chandler (1864–1945) with his most famous project, the "re-creation" of Revere's home, as many architects of his pre-Modern generation were well versed in a variety of styles. Chandler was trained at M.I.T. He also restored the Old Corner Bookstore in Boston and the House of Seven Gables in Salem. Chandler's commission list, as documented by Orwig, contained more than five hundred projects, with several houses near Dublin – in Temple, Jaffrey, and including the summer house of Governor Robert P. Bass in Peterborough (1913–15); he also drew up restoration plans for naval historian Samuel Eliot Morison's family home, Bleakhouse, in Peterborough (1928).

A longtime owner of the Newbegin house (more recently called Blueberry Hill, although Chandler refers to it as Blueberry Patch), Mrs. Ellen B. Ballou was a historian and author of *The Building of the House* (1970), a history of the Boston publisher, Houghton Mifflin.

Historic New England owns a drawing titled "Study Revision of House at Dublin, N.H.," dated 27 Nov. 1933, which shows a dwelling that is not unlike the Newbegin house in its Anglo picturesqueness. This design of Frank Chouteau Brown (1876–1947), a Bostonian noted for his large country estates and books on English and American architecture (*New England Houses* [1919] and *Modern English Churches* [1923], for example), depicts a fascinating mélange of English Tudor and American Colonial elements. There is a tall, narrow central section that recalls a house in an English medieval town; it has both leaded panes and 6-over-6 sashes, and it projects over a drive that cuts through the house. Spreading out from this is a living room block featuring a polygonal bay gabled with half-timbering. Attached to this is a somewhat simpler, more American-looking service wing. Because Brown labels the gatehouse and the living room sections as "Old. Bldg.," one supposes that this house already existed. Or, was it a fancy on the part of the imaginative Brown? Brown was an editor of the Society for the Preservation of New England Antiquities' journal *Old-Time New England*, as well as an administrator for the Historic American Buildings Survey in Massachusetts. Chandler biographer Orwig notes that while Chandler knew Brown professionally, there is no connection between the projects.

14 Kent had been a student of Thayer and it was he who invited Robeson to sing at the James studio, during the summer of 1922 when Robeson was in Peterborough acting in Eugene O'Neill's *The Emperor Jones* at Mariarden; Robeson was also a visitor at Loon Point (Duffy Monahon, "Peterborough, Cradle of the Arts," *Monadnock Ledger*, [23 Jan. 1986]; Monahon wrote that Robeson possibly also sang at Pompelia and at George Luther Foote's). Robeson also stayed at the Jameses, as he remarked to his hosts that it was the only time he had spent the night in a white person's house (the Dublin Historical Society owns Mrs. Robeson's thank-you letter to the Jameses).

Besides the members of the extended family, including Henry James, T. S. Eliot was brought to tea by his brother, Henry, while staying at his cousin Aimée Lamb's in 1946. Lamb, a Boston painter, lived in the Piper-Derby house on Main Street and had studied with Thayer and Alexander James. Lamb was the niece of architect Arthur Rotch, and served for twenty-five years as the president of the Rotch Traveling Scholarship. The Italian government knighted Lamb "in recognition of her efforts to make the architectural treasures of Italy become a living tradition in America."

15 The studio is now the home of Alexander James's grandson, the painter and photographer, Christopher James.

16 Gugler's obituary in *The New York Post* (17 May 1974) ran to only 60 words. The 1965 Franklin Roosevelt memorial on Roosevelt Island in the Potomac has been superseded by a larger landscape and sculpture park, although the plain stone and marble block suited F.D.R., who wished for nothing more than a simple marker in Washington. Gugler created the granite base for Manship's bronze sculpture of Theodore Roosevelt (1967), also in Washington. Gugler's piano case for the White House was patented by Steinway in 1938.

17 Alexander James died less than a year after the studio's completion, but his widow Frederika, an artist herself and President of the Herb Society of America, made it a center of artists in Dublin and the entire region through fairs, cultural events, and exhibitions (including the work of her sculptor son Michael). In October of 1965, the James Studio was the site of the Second Dublin Peace Conference. There is a local legend that Kennedy and Soviet premier Nikita Khrushchev met secretly at the James Studio while Kennedy was president. Christopher James recalls his grandmother Freddie telling him of the meeting, which he says was arranged by Grenville Clark (interview, 26 August 2009).

Eric Gugler designed a house for the actress Katherine Cornell on Martha's Vineyard (1937–1945) that features massive barn-like beams in the main room.

18 Mary Pierce was trained by both her father and Thayer, and she served as the model for many of Brush's paintings, including *In the Garden* (Metropolitan Museum). She was married (and widowed) three times: to the inventor Winslow Pierce, the artist William James, Jr. (son of the philosopher and older brother of Alexander), and Grenville Clark.

Another studio was built after the James and Pierce ones, when architect William Campbell designed a house and separate studio about 1957 for his wife Barbara, the daughter of sculptor George Grey Barnard, on Learned Road.

"Handy" Cabot, too, came from an important local family; his wife Thea was a daughter of Brush. He was the grandson of Raphael Pumpelly and of Thomas Handasyd Cabot, a friend of Emerson and the partner of Boston architect Edward C. Cabot, designer of the Louis Cabot home on Windmill Hill Road. His help with the design and construction of Stone House demonstrated his ability to build attractive and substantial appearing houses with limited means and the simplest of materials. Cabot (1904–1983) was a graduate of Harvard and worked in the technical metals business when Mary Brush Pierce brought him to New Hampshire to help remodel a house in Hancock. In addition to Stone House and the concrete block Pink House for Mabel Bremer (later the wife of Episcopal Bishop J. D. Larned) on Windmill Hill Road, Cabot designed another block house on Lake Road, about 1953, and his only frame house for author Edith Roelker Curtis, about 1958. Cabot's last work was for Governor (later Senator) John Chaffee in East Greenwich, R.I.

CHAPTER NINE

1   The Lehmanns founded the Dublin School in 1935. The school did not adopt this style for later structures. In a number of buildings designed in the 1960s by Charles La Roche, a builder from Peterborough, it attempted an economical sort of Modernism. The Main Office/Science Building (1961), the new dormitory (1964), and the Art Studio (1967) have low roofs, large areas of glass, and a somewhat insipid Formalist character. In 1981 the school returned to the Shingle Style roots of some early buildings by employing Richard Monahon, who designed a Postmodern addition to the Hart house.

The eighteenth-century cottage style survives in Dublin: an advertisement in *The Peterborough Transcript* (28 Mar. 1985) shows a smaller version of the School House, which is labeled a "New Dublin Cape."

2   The paradigm of the contemporary pre-fab home is the mobile home, or trailer, of which there is at least one in Dublin. In 1981, a fifth of all new homes in the United States were trailers. Despite the technology available to industrial pre-fabricators, most of these are flimsy metal boxes, and mobile only in that they are rolled fully built onto their sites. Because they are relatively inexpensive, trailers became associated with poverty and the lower classes (Keene writer Ernest Hebert's 1979 book *The Dogs of March* includes some "trailer trash" who live in a trailer in a fictional town that is in part modeled on Dublin); some Monadnock region towns have sought to exclude them.

3   The Cambridge School of Architecture was for women students, although the teachers also served on the faculty at Harvard's Graduate School of Design. Raymond, who opened her own firm in 1928 and who died in 1989, was the subject of a monograph by Doris Cole, *Eleanor Raymond, Architect* (Philadelphia: 1981). The Chapin house is not among the architect's works listed in the book, nor is it or another work included in the list of Raymond's works in *The First American Women Architects* by Sarah Allaback (Urbana: 2008), 183–188; this reference work has a short bibliography on Raymond. Her second Dublin commission was a renovation for William K. and Katharine Mitchell Jackson at Stonewall Farm off Page Road in 1949; Raymond had designed the Jacksons' winter home in the Boston suburb of Chestnut Hill (Katharine Mitchell was the sister of the controversial World War I aviator, Billy Mitchell). Raymond donated her papers to the Frances Loeb Library at the Harvard School of Design.

4   "My uncle [Michael 'Micky' James] is confident that Dad [Alexander James] started at Harvard and transferred to Yale. Micky makes a reference to Dad 'going off to Yale in February' in his last entry (31 Jan. 1945) of his WWII diary. So Dad must have started at Harvard in the fall of 1944." Henry James, e-mail to author, 12 December 2009. Yale University archivist, Rebecca Hatcher, confirmed that the Catalogue of Graduates lists James

"as having received a Bachelor of Architecture degree in 1948." Hatcher, e-mail to author, 11 December 2009.

5 Dave Weinstein, "Flamboyant modernism: Henry Hill's stellar taste and love for the arts is reflected in the homes he designed," *San Francisco Chronicle* (11 June 2005).

6 Alexander James' own house of 1956–57 was built above the lake, very close to where Abbott Thayer's 1888 house and studio stood (they were demolished in the 1930s). Nearby, on Lake Road, Boston architect James Hopkins enlarged Mrs. Copley Greene's Lilac Cottage of c. 1900 in 1958. Ten years later, Pittsfield, Massachusetts architect Terry Halleck built a contemporary house next door.

   Upon learning that his friend and fellow architect Robert A.M. Stern was going to Dublin for a visit, Philip Johnson remarked: "Dublin! Oh my God! All those trees! There's nothing in Dublin but trees." Told to the author by Stern, Dublin, 21 July 1982. Johnson, along with historian Henry-Russell Hitchcock, created the term International Style in 1932 as the label for an exhibition they mounted at the Museum of Modern Art.

7 James Hilleary, a graduate of Catholic University, is best known for his color-field paintings. Smith went to Dartmouth, was an Olympic athlete, and an Air Force pilot. After a successful career as an oilman, Smith began collecting glass from all historical periods; his collection eventually went to the Smithsonian and to the Corning Museum (see *Glass from the Ancient World: The Ray Winfield Smith Collection*, Corning Museum, [1957]). Working with the University of Pennsylvania Museum, Smith helped document the Temple of Nefertiti in Aswan, Egypt.

8 James Hilleary, telephone interview, 18 December 2008.

   Oak Hill was given to Dartmouth College in 1976 (Smith had hoped it would become an institute for the study of glass); the following year it was sold to Constantine and L. Joyce Hampers. Dr. Hampers was one of the developers of the kidney dialysis machine, while Mrs. Hampers is the former Massachusetts Commissioner of Revenue.

9 Richard Bancker McCurdy prepared for Yale at Hotchkiss. By 1995, McCurdy had left Branford for Santa Fe, New Mexico, where he listed himself as "Architect, Developer." He remembers wanting to be an architect from the age of fourteen. An older brother collected imitation stone German blocks called Richter's Anchor (Anker) Blocks, which captured McCurdy's imagination, and he never looked back.

10 Telephone interview with Richard McCurdy, 18 September 2009.

11 The firm of Sherwood, Mills & Smith (later called SMS) was founded in 1946 and became one of the largest architectural firms in Connecticut. Founder Willis N. Mills, Sr., was a classmate of Louis Kahn's at the University of Pennsylvania. Mills, Jr., designer of the two Dublin houses, did family housing for the United States Air Force following completion of architecture school at Princeton.

12 The Burnham house garnered two full pages in a book published by *Architectural Record* in 1976 called *Great Houses*, and titled "A Contemporary Farmhouse in New England" (54–55). The authors note that the house evokes the "austere, four-square self-sufficiency of the traditional American farmhouse." Furthermore, "the problems facing those who build in northern [sic] New Hampshire have not changed in two hundred years." The diagonal siding, according to the writers, ties "the building to the land and thrusts the matching half-gables to the sky."

13 Moore was also responsible for the house's enlargement in 1974, while Daniel Scully added a kitchen, dining room, bedroom, and office in 1991. Allen Moore, Jr. is a native of Nashville, went to

154

the Kent School, and was graduated from Yale College in the class of 1956; he received a graduate degree in architecture from Yale two years later. Along the way, he managed to spend a year studying in Rome and set up a Caribbean practice based on the island of St. Croix in the American Virgin Islands. Moore also opened an office in Cambridge, and more recently, Newburyport. He was involved in the planning of the national park based around the mills in Lowell, and he designed the headquarters for Ocean Spray Cranberries, beating out Walter Gropius' firm of The Architects Collaborative to win the commission. Moore's most distinguished work is the National Yiddish Book Center at Hampshire College, in Amherst, Massachusetts (1997, 2007).

14 Acorn was founded in 1947 by John Bemis, an associate of Karl Koch; Bemis studied architecture and building construction at M.I.T. Deck House was founded in 1959 by Gropius disciple William Berkes. The two companies merged in 1995. Under the name Empyrean, the company continued to be a pioneer in pre-fabricated houses until 2009.

15 The addition to Morelands, now called Red Top, is amply illustrated in the Rizzoli monograph, *Robert A.M. Stern, 1965–1980: Toward a Modern Architecture after Modernism* (Peter Arnell and Ted Bickford, eds., [New York: 1982]). Stern is now the dean of the architecture school at Yale.

16 The Thayer house is technically just over the line into Harrisville, but it can be considered part of the Dublin colony. Monahon is responsible for several smaller but equally sensitive renovations and additions in Dublin, such as the 1981–82 remodeling of the Eveleth Cottage on Burpee Road for Bruce McClellan, former headmaster of the Lawrenceville School, and the 1982 additions to the William Raymond house on Learned Road. (See William Morgan, "Alumni Profile: Richard Monahon," *Dartmouth Alumni Magazine* [October 1987]).

17 Judd Hale, e-mail to author, 15 October 2009.

18 Scully's house is illustrated in "House Dreams," *New England Monthly*, Vol. 2 (June 1985), 54–55. See also, Rachel Carley, "'Highway 101,' Architect's Home, Is Almost a Car," *New York Times* [13 Nov. 1986], C1; "A Man's Home Is His Chassis," *Americana* (Feb. 1987), 88; Daniel V. Scully, "Morning Thunder on Highway 101: An Emblematic Tale about Architecture," *Global Architecture Houses* 29 (1990). Scully's house was also featured in *Ripley's Believe It or Not!* ("It auto drive car buffs wild. Dan Scully, an auto buff and architect of Dublin, N.H., constructed his home in the shape of a car and dubbed it Highway 101 – Two Lane Blacktop," [7 July 1987]). Scully is the subject of a portrait, "The Flaneur of the Strip," in Howard Mansfield's *The Bones of the Earth* (Berkeley: 2004). Scully uses the garage to prepare classic Volvo race cars.

An example of Scully's non-"Carchitecture" is the modern interpretation of a Shingle Style cottage that he designed for Alexa Thayer, a painter and graphic designer, just over the line in Harrisville. (See William Morgan, "Daniel Scully in Dublin New Hampshire," *Art New England* [October/November 2000].) The small house features a large round window that frames a view of the mountain – an echo of the moon gate at the Joseph Lindon Smith's Loon Point of a century earlier.

19 Susan Barker, e-mail to author, 31 December 2009.

THIS BOOK'S genealogy can be traced to a 1976 Bicentennial project of the Dublin Conservation Commission. A survey of the town's buildings resulted in the nomination of more than 150 structures and two historic districts to the National Register of Historic Places – a nomination that was accepted in 1983. William L. Bauhan wrote most of the history and I contributed the architectural analysis.

Over the years, a great deal has been written about Dublin's growth and development from a farming community into a nationally known summer resort. A town history, written by the Rev. Levi Leonard in 1855 and updated by the Rev. Josiah Seward in 1920, exceeds 1,000 pages. Henry Darracott Allison's memoir, *Dublin Days Old and New*, appeared during the town's bicentennial in 1952. Tom Hyman prepared a new town history in 2002, while Richard Meryman's 2001 history of the Dublin Lake Club covered the summer colony's social life. Thus, it seems appropriate that this volume should focus on Dublin's built environment.

This book owes its existence to the extraordinary support of the Dublin Historical Society. Thanks to members, board, and staff – particularly Nancy Campbell and John Harris. Sarah Bauhan and Henry James joined forces with John Harris to ensure that this book would be finished and published.

They were assisted by dozens of welcoming and helpful Dublin property owners and summer residents. The historical society's archivist, John Harris, and his conservationist wife Betsey provided unfailingly gracious hospitality at Stonewall Farm. It was Dan Scully who insisted that I revive a fallow architectural study and make it a book; he offered constant constructive criticism and a second home for me in Dublin.

The Allen R. Hite Art Institute of the University of Louisville was my academic home during much of the Dublin book project. Architectural historians and visiting professors at Louisville, Leonard Eaton of the University of Michigan and the late John Coolidge of Harvard, read the manuscript at an early stage. The National Endowment for the Humanities awarded me both a summer grant and a senior fellowship to further research on this architectural history.

Living as he does in Mark Twain's summer home, publisher David R. Godine has an especial insight into the magic of Dublin, and he understood the value of making this history available. He and Carl W. Scarbrough shepherded the ideas and images into a handsome book.

Long association with Dublin has meant that my family has endured many trips to the mountain when they might have wished to be elsewhere. Yet, the now-grown children remember the place fondly, and I like to believe that the spirit of the mountain is a part of them. My wife Carolyn has shared the at-times seemingly endless saga of "the book." The successful appearance of *Monadnock Summer* is a testament to her.

WILLIAM MORGAN
Providence, Rhode Island

156 Nancy Belluscio 48, 127 (top); Foote Family 55; David R. Godine 78; Dublin Historical Society 2, 15, 20, 24, 25 (left), 32 (top), 33, 34, 39, 40–41, 44, 45, 49, 51, 52, 53, 59, 60, 67, 68, 70, 72 (left), 73, 75 (right), 81, 82, 83, 86, 87, 89, 92, 93, 94 (right), 95, 96, 98, 101, 102, 107, 108; Dublin Public Library 14, 16, 17, 26, 27, 30, 31, 32 (bottom and right), 37, 38, 46, 47, 52 (bottom right), 56, 58, 61, 94 (left); James Hillerary 118; Historical Society of Cheshire County 36, 90; Historic New England 69; Richard B. McCurdy 119; Richard Meryman 74, 85, 97 (right), 97; William Morgan 1, 8, 12, 18, 19, 21, 22, 23, 25 (right), 28, 29, 43, 50, 54, 62, 64, 71, 72 (right), 75 (left), 76, 79, 80, 85 (left), 88, 91, 99, 100, 105, 106, 109, 110, 111, 112, 114, 116, 120, 121, 123, 127 (bottom), 128; Whitney Morrill 130; David Reeve 125, 126 ; Paul Rocheleau 124.

A NOTE ON THE TYPE

MONADNOCK SUMMER has been set in Quadraat, a type designed in 1992 by Fred Smeijers. The original designs for Quadraat combined Renaissance elegance with current ideas on construction and form, resulting in a fresh interpretation of historical models that, because it is not a revival or reinterpretation of any single existing type, is especially well suited to the typographic needs of contemporary designers. First released as a serif face, the family has since been expanded to include sans-serif and display styles. As a family, the Quadraat types possess a distinct, recognizable appearance without being aggressively or unsuitably decorative.

DESIGN & COMPOSITION BY CARL W. SCARBROUGH